MASTERING AI WITH PYTHON

A Beginner's Guide to Navigating the AI Revolution

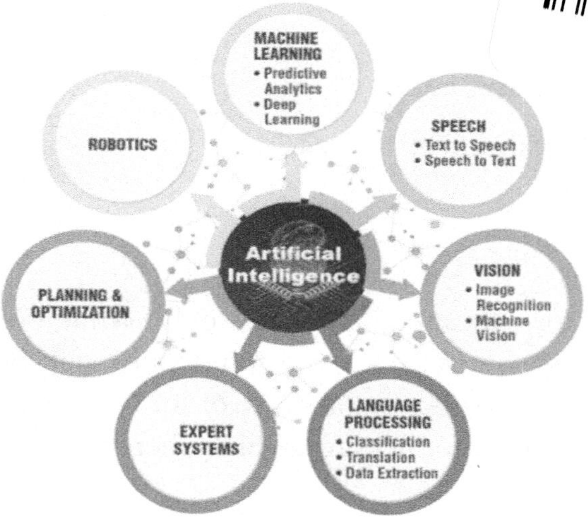

Machine Learning, Deep Learning,

Agentic AI, GenAI, LLM

python

Author: Ghulam Mustafa

Publisher: VertixCloud, London

Mastering AI with Python:

A Beginner's Guide to Navigating the AI Revolution

Published by **VertixCloud**

ISBN: 978-1-9195004-0-9 (Paperback)

www.vertixcloud.com

First Edition – 2026

For permissions or inquiries, email: support@vertixcloud.com

Inside this book, you'll learn:

✓ Python for AI — From Zero to Ready

Set up your environment, learn core Python basics, and work with essential data science libraries like NumPy, Pandas, Matplotlib, Scikit-learn, and TensorFlow.

✓ Machine Learning Made Simple

Explore supervised and unsupervised learning, build your first ML models, understand regression and classification, and apply evaluation metrics like a pro.

✓ Deep Learning & Neural Networks

Discover how neural networks work, build models with Keras, train CNNs for image recognition, LSTMs for text data, and understand the architecture behind modern AI systems.

✓ Generative AI, Transformers & LLMs

Understand how GPT, BERT, and Transformer models work, learn prompt engineering, work with Hugging Face, and build your own text generation projects.

✓ AI Agents & The Future of Intelligence

Dive into the next evolution of AI—autonomous agents that plan, reason, and act. Build your first agent using frameworks like LangChain and explore the future of AI + robotics + edge computing.

Who is this book for?

This book is designed for:

- Beginners with zero AI experience
- Python developers entering the AI/ML world
- Students and professionals exploring AI careers
- Anyone curious about how AI systems actually work
- Tech enthusiasts building real AI projects

No prior machine learning or deep learning knowledge is required—just curiosity and a willingness to learn.

What makes this book different?

- **Beginner-friendly explanations** without oversimplifying
- **Hands-on projects** in every section
- **Modern coverage** including Transformers, Generative AI, LLMs, and AI Agents
- **Clear learning path** from fundamentals to real-world applications
- **Written in 2026 for the modern AI landscape, this book reflects the latest advancements in AI, LLMs, and agent-based systems.**

Start your journey into Artificial Intelligence today.

With this book as your guide, you'll gain the skills, confidence, and understanding needed to build AI applications and thrive in the AI-driven future.

MASTERING AI WITH PYTHON

A Beginner's Guide to Navigating the AI Revolution

Table of contents:

PART I – GETTING STARTED WITH PYTHON 1

Chapter 1: Introduction to Artificial Intelligence 2

1.1 Why Learn AI Development Today? 3

1.2 Why Python Is the Best Language for AI? 4

1.3 What You'll Learn and Build in This Book 5

Chapter 2: Setting Up Python for AI 6

2.1 Installing Python 7

2.2 Choosing Development Tools 7

2.3 Working with Jupyter Notebook and Google Colab 8

2.4 Essential Python Libraries for AI 10

2.5 Testing Your Python Environment 11

Chapter 3: Python Basics for AI Development 13

3.1 How Python Is Used in AI Development 13

3.2 Python Syntax and Structure 14

3.3 Variables, Data Types, and Expressions 15

3.4 Python Data Structures 16

3.5 Conditional Statements and Loops 17

3.6 Functions and Modules 18

3.7 Python Coding Best Practices 19

Chapter 4: Working with NumPy, Pandas, Matplotlib for AI....21
4.1 Introduction....21
4.2 NumPy for Numerical Computing....23
4.3 Pandas for Data Manipulation....25
4.4 Matplotlib for Data Visualization....28
4.5 Summary....32
PART II – ARTIFICIAL INTELLIGENCE & MACHINE LEARNING....33
Chapter 5: What Is Artificial Intelligence?....34
5.1 Introduction....34
5.2 AI vs Machine Learning vs Deep Learning....35
5.3 Real-World Applications of AI....37
5.4 The AI Application Workflow....39
5.5 Summary....41
Chapter 6: Introduction to Machine Learning....42
6.1 What Is Machine Learning?....42
6.2 Types of Machine Learning....43
6.3 Core Machine Learning Concepts....45
6.4 Popular Machine Learning Algorithms....46
6.5 Introduction to scikit-learn....47
6.6 Hands-On: Building Your First Machine Learning Model 48
6.7 Summary....50
Chapter 7: Supervised Learning with Python....51
7.1 What Is Supervised Learning?....51
7.2 How Supervised Learning Works....53

7.3 Regression: Predicting Continuous Values 54
7.4 Classification: Predicting Categories 57
7.5 Evaluating Model Performance 60
7.6 Comparing and Selecting Models....................................... 61
7.7 Saving and Using Trained Models 62
7.8 Hands-On: Predicting House Prices using Supervised Learning 62
7.9 Summary 65
Chapter 8: Unsupervised Learning with Python 66
8.1 What Is Unsupervised Learning? 66
8.2 How Unsupervised Learning Works 68
8.3 Clustering: Grouping Similar Data Points 69
8.4 Dimensionality Reduction: Simplifying Complex Data..... 73
8.5 Evaluation of Unsupervised Models 74
8.6 Hands-On Project: Customer Segmentation using Unsupervised Learning.. 75
8.7 Summary 78
PART III – DEEP LEARNING & NEURAL NETWORKS 79
Chapter 9: Introduction to Neural Networks & Deep Learning . 80
9.1 What Are Neural Networks & Deep Learning 81
9.2 How Neural Networks Learn 84
9.3 When to Use Deep Learning 86
9.4 Introduction to TensorFlow and Keras.............................. 89
9.5 Hands-On: Building Your First Neural Network with Keras 91
9.6 Summary 94

Chapter 10: Building and Training Deep Learning Models 95
10.1 Understanding Deep Learning Architectures 95
10.2 Training Concepts: Layers, Epochs, Batches and Hyperparameters 97
10.3 Loss Functions and Optimizers 99
10.4 Activation Functions 101
10.5 Evaluating Model Performance 102
10.6 Hands-On: Building a Deep Neural Network with Keras 105
10.7 Saving, Loading & Reusing Models 108
10.8 Summary 109
Chapter 11: Advanced Neural Network Architectures 110
11.1 Convolutional Neural Networks (CNNs) 110
11.2 Convolution, Pooling & Feature Extraction 111
11.3 Hands-On: Image Classification with a CNN 114
11.4 Recurrent Neural Networks (RNNs) 117
11.5 When to Use CNNs vs RNNs 119
11.6 Summary 120
PART IV – AGENTIC AI, GENERATIVE AI & LARGE LANGUAGE MODELS 121
Chapter 12: Generative AI & Autoencoders 122
12.1 What Is Generative AI? 122
12.2 Discriminative vs. Generative Models 125
12.3 Autoencoders 128
12.4 GANs: Generative Adversarial Networks 129
12.5 Hands-On Project: Image Generation with a GAN 131

12.6 Ethical Considerations and Deepfake Awareness 134

12.7 Summary 137

Chapter 13: Large Language Models & Prompt Engineering .. 138

13.1 Transformers: The NLP Revolution 138

13.2 How Attention and Self-Attention Work 141

13.3 Large Language Model Architectural Overview 144

13.4 How LLMs Are Trained and Fine-Tuned 148

13.5 Prompt Engineering: Techniques and Best Practices 151

13.6 Hands-On: Generate Text with a Pre-Trained GPT Model from Hugging Face 153

13.7 Real-World Applications of Large Language Models.... 158

13.8 Summary 160

Chapter 14: Agentic AI and the Future of Intelligence 161

14.1 What Is Agentic AI? 161

14.2 How AI Agents Plan, Reason and Act Autonomously ... 164

14.3 Agent Components: Tools, Memory & Context 168

14.4 Agents External Knowledge & Long-Term Memory...... 172

14.4.1 What Is RAG (Retrieval-Augmented Generation)? 175

14.4.2 MCP (Model Context Protocol) vs RAG 178

14.5 Agents Frameworks - LangChain, AutoGen, CrewAI... 181

14.6 Hands-On: Build Your First Autonomous AI Agent 185

14.7 The Future: AI + Robotics + Edge Computing 188

14.8 Hands-On: Build your RAG AI Agent - PDF Q&A Chatbot using LangChain and OpenAI 190

14.9 Summary 197

Chapter 15: Final Summary & Next Steps 198
15.1 What You've Learned in This Book 198
15.2 Building Your Own AI Projects 200
15.3 Exploring Career Opportunities in AI 203
15.4 Career Paths & Opportunities in AI 205
15.5 Continuing Your Learning Journey 209
AUTHOR'S NOTE: 213
ABOUT THE AUTHOR 214
ABOUT VERTIXCLOUD 215

Part I – Getting Started with Python

Chapter 1: Introduction to Artificial Intelligence

Artificial Intelligence (AI) is no longer a distant or experimental technology—it is already shaping how software is built, how businesses operate, and how people interact with technology every day. From recommendation systems and intelligent chatbots to self-driving cars and generative models that create text, images, and code, AI has become one of the most influential forces in modern computing.

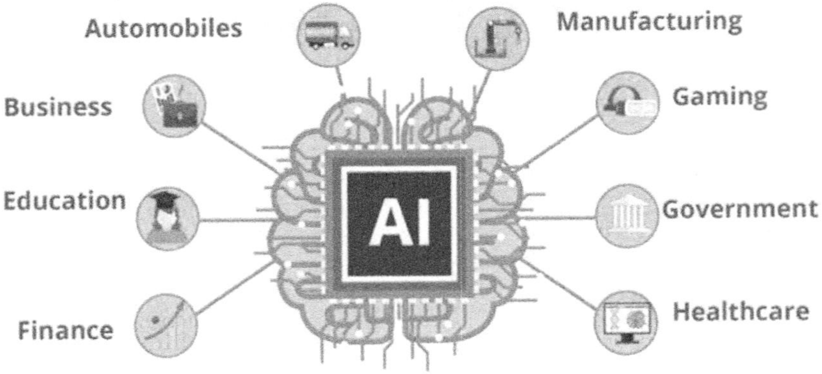

This book is designed to give you a **clear, practical, and beginner-friendly path into AI using Python**. Rather than focusing on heavy mathematics or abstract theory, you'll learn AI by building real understanding step by step—starting from Python fundamentals and gradually moving into more advanced concepts.

As you progress through this book, you will explore **Machine Learning**, where models learn patterns from data to make predictions and decisions. You'll then move into **Neural Networks and Deep Learning**, understanding how modern AI systems learn complex representations using layered architectures. From there, the book introduces **Generative AI**, including models that can generate text, images, and other content, along with the core ideas behind Transformers and Large Language Models (LLMs).

You will also learn about the next evolution of AI systems: **Agentic AI**. These systems go beyond prediction and generation—they can plan, reason, use tools, retrieve external knowledge, and act autonomously to achieve goals. By the later chapters, you'll understand how modern AI agents work and how they are built using contemporary frameworks.

By the end of this book, you won't just understand what Artificial Intelligence is—you'll understand **how it works, why it works, and how to build AI-powered systems using Python**. Whether you are a beginner, a Python developer expanding into AI, or a professional exploring the modern AI landscape, this book is designed to give you both confidence and practical skills for the AI-driven future.

1.1 Why Learn AI Development Today?

Artificial Intelligence (AI) is transforming the world around us—from personalized recommendations on Netflix and Amazon, to self-driving cars, fraud detection, and intelligent chatbots. As the demand for AI-powered solutions grows, so does the need for skilled professionals who can build and implement these technologies.

1.2 Why Python Is the Best Language for AI?

Among the many programming languages available today, **Python** has emerged as the leading choice for AI and machine learning development.

Here are several reasons why:

Simplicity and Readability: Python's clean and human-readable syntax makes it easy for beginners to pick up quickly. It reduces the complexity of coding so that you can focus more on solving problems and less on writing boilerplate code.

Rich Ecosystem of Libraries: Python offers a wide array of libraries and frameworks specifically designed for AI, including NumPy, Pandas, Scikit-learn, TensorFlow, Keras, PyTorch, LangChain and many more. These tools handle everything from numerical computing and data manipulation to training deep neural networks.

Community Support: Python has a vast and active global community. Whether you're troubleshooting a problem or exploring a new library, you're likely to find tutorials, documentation, and open-source code to help you out.

Flexibility and Integration: Python integrates well with other programming languages and platforms, which makes it a versatile tool in AI pipelines. You can easily connect Python with web applications, databases, cloud services and big data systems.

Proven Track Record in AI: Leading tech companies and research institutions use Python for cutting-edge AI projects. From Google and Facebook to NASA and MIT, Python is trusted across industries.

1.3 What You'll Learn and Build in This Book

In this book, we'll take you on a journey through the world of AI using Python—from the basics of coding to building your own intelligent systems. Whether you're an aspiring developer, a student, or a professional looking to reskill, this guide is designed to help you build a strong foundation and start creating meaningful AI projects.

Let's dive in and begin your journey toward **mastering AI with Python!**

Chapter 2:
Setting Up Python for AI

Before we dive into artificial intelligence and machine learning, it's important to set up a Python development environment. In this chapter, we'll introduce three most commonly used tools for AI development—**Jupyter Notebook, Visual Studio Code (VS Code) and Google Colab**, a free cloud-based Jupyter Notebook environment.

For simplicity and ease of learning, all examples in this book will be demonstrated using **Jupyter Notebook or Google Colab**.

By the end of this chapter, you will have:

- Installed Python on your computer.
- Learned how to use **Jupyter Notebook** (a popular tool for data science and AI coding).
- Explored **Google Colab**, a cloud-based alternative that provides free GPU access.
- Installed the most important AI libraries: **NumPy, Pandas, Matplotlib, Scikit-learn, TensorFlow** and **LangChain.**

Let's get started.

2.1 Installing Python

Python is the backbone of AI development. Most AI frameworks, including TensorFlow and LangChain, are built with Python support.

Step 1: Check if Python is installed

- On Windows: Open Command Prompt and type:

```
python -version
```

- On macOS/Linux: Open Terminal and type:

```
python3 -version
```

Step 2: Download Python

- Visit python.org and download the latest Python 3 version.

Step 3: Install and Configure PATH

- On Windows, check the box **"Add Python to PATH"** during installation to avoid manual configuration.

2.2 Choosing Development Tools

An **IDE (Integrated Development Environment)** is a tool where you write and execute code. Three popular options for AI development are:

- **Jupyter Notebook**: Best for beginners and data analysis. You can run code cell-by-cell and see results immediately, making it perfect for experimentation.
- **Visual Studio Code**: A powerful code editor suitable for more complex projects. It supports Jupyter notebooks as well, but we will mainly focus on Jupyter or Colab for this book.
- **Google Colab:** A free cloud Jupyter Notebook that runs in your browser and gives you temporary access to powerful hardware GPUs to train AI models.

For this book, you can use **Jupyter Notebook or Google Colab**. As you progress, you may explore VS Code for more complex projects.

2.3 Working with Jupyter Notebook and Google Colab

2.3.1 Jupyter Notebook:

Jupyter Notebooks allow you to write and execute Python code interactively, making them perfect for learning and experimenting with AI concepts.

Step 1: Install Jupyter

```
pip install notebook
```

Step 2: Launch Jupyter

```
jupyter notebook
```

This command will open a browser window where you can create and manage notebooks for your AI projects.

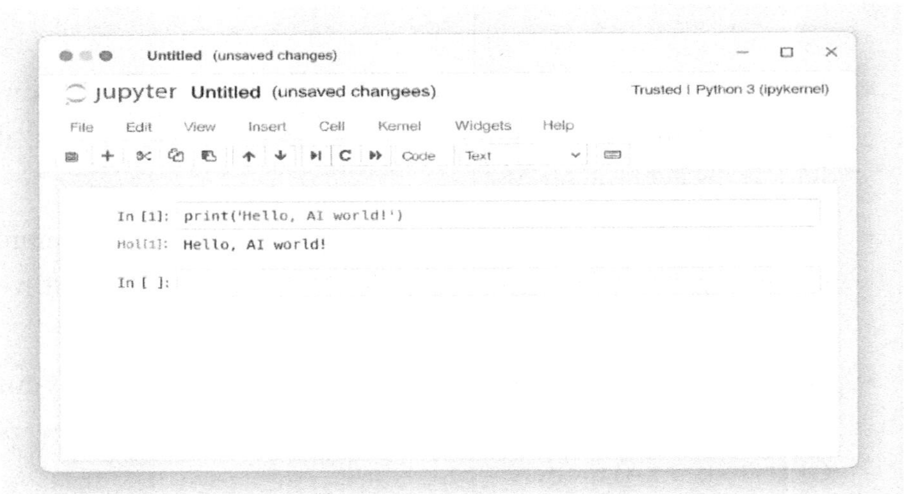

2.3.2 Google Colab:

Google Colab (short for *Collaboratory*) is a free, cloud-based Jupyter Notebook environment provided by Google. It allows you to write and run Python code directly in your web browser—no installation, no setup, and no need for a powerful computer.

Why use Google Colab?

- **No installation required** — everything runs online in the cloud.
- **Works on any device** — Windows, macOS, Linux, or even tablets.
- **Built-in GPU/TPU acceleration** — ideal for AI and deep learning training.
- **Pre-installed AI libraries** — Including NumPy, Pandas, Matplotlib, TensorFlow, PyTorch, Scikit-learn, and more.
- **Seamless notebook experience** — same interface as Jupyter Notebook.
- **Automatic saving in Google Drive** — your notebooks stay synced and backed up.

Getting Started with Colab:

1. Go to: https://colab.google.com
2. Sign in with your Google account.
3. Click **New Notebook** to create your first cloud-based Jupyter environment.

2.4 Essential Python Libraries for AI

Python becomes powerful for AI when combined with the right libraries. Let's install the following essential libraries for AI development in Python:

NumPy: (Fast Numerical Computations)

NumPy (Numerical Python) is fundamental for scientific computing with Python. It provides support for large, multi-dimensional arrays and matrices, along with a collection of high-level mathematical functions to operate on these arrays.

Pandas: (Data Manipulation and Analysis)

Pandas is widely used for data manipulation and analysis, Pandas makes it easy to work with datasets (tables, CSV files, etc.). It introduces powerful data structures namely the Series (a one-dimensional array-like object) and the DataFrame (a two-dimensional table, like a spreadsheet).

Matplotlib: (Data Visualization)

Matplotlib lets you create graphs and plots to visualize your data and model results. It is highly customizable for creating static, interactive, and animated visualizations in Python.

Scikit-learn:(Machine Learning Models)

Scikit-learn is widely used for machine learning in Python. It provides a consistent, simple interface to a comprehensive range of supervised and unsupervised learning algorithms. It includes methods for classification, regression, clustering, and dimensionality reduction, as well as tools for model selection and evaluation.

TensorFlow:(Deep Learning Framework)

TensorFlow is Google's open-source library, is one of the leading frameworks for deep learning. This library enables developers to construct and train large-scale neural networks with multiple layers, making it the primary tool for building, training, and deploying deep learning models across a variety of applications.

LangChain:(AI Agents and LLM Framework)

LangChain is one of the earliest and most widely used frameworks for AI agents and LLM-powered applications. It provides all the core components needed to build autonomous systems.

Install Essential Python Libraries on your local machine:

```
pip install numpy pandas matplotlib
pip install scikit-learn tensorflow langchain
```

2.5 Testing Your Python Environment

To confirm that everything is working correctly, create a new Jupyter notebook and run the following code:

```
import numpy as np
import pandas as pd
import matplotlib as plt
import sklearn
import tensorflow as tf
import langchain

print("All libraries installed successfully!")
```

If no errors appear, congratulations—you're ready to dive into AI development with Python.

2.5.1 Tips for Beginners

Here are some helpful tips as you start using Jupyter Notebook:

- Name your notebooks clearly (e.g., chapter1_setup.ipynb).
- Save your work frequently to avoid losing progress.
- Use **Markdown cells** to add notes or explanations alongside your code.
- Keep your notebooks organized in separate folders for each chapter or project.

2.5.2 Summary

You now have a fully functional Python environment using **Jupyter Notebook** and **Google Colab**. All examples in this book can be run in either environment. In the next chapter, we'll cover Python basics to ensure you have a solid foundation before diving deeper into machine learning and artificial intelligence.

Chapter 3:
Python Basics for AI Development

Before building machine learning models or neural networks, it's essential to be comfortable with Python's core programming concepts. AI development relies heavily on clean code, data manipulation, and logical flow, all of which are built on strong Python fundamentals.

In this chapter, you'll learn the Python basics that are most relevant to AI and data-driven applications. Rather than covering every aspect of the language, the focus is on concepts you will repeatedly use when working with datasets, implementing algorithms, and building AI pipelines. You'll explore variables, data types, control flow, functions, and essential data structures such as lists and dictionaries.

By the end of this chapter, you'll have a solid foundation in Python programming and be ready to work confidently with libraries like NumPy and Pandas in the next chapters.

3.1 How Python Is Used in AI Development

In AI development, Python serves as the language that connects data, models, and applications. While the underlying AI concepts may involve complex mathematics, Python is the tool developers use to turn those ideas into working systems.

Python is commonly used to **prepare and process data** before training models. Developers load datasets, clean and transform data, and organize it into formats suitable for machine learning and deep learning. This preparation step is critical, as model performance depends heavily on data quality.

Python is also central to **training and experimenting with AI models**. Using Python libraries, developers define models, train them on data, adjust parameters, and evaluate results. Small changes in code make it easy to experiment and improve performance.

Finally, Python is widely used to **integrate and deploy AI solutions**. Models trained in Python can be embedded into applications, APIs, and automated workflows, allowing AI systems to move from experimentation to real-world use.

This practical role of Python explains why a solid understanding of the language's fundamentals is essential before diving deeper into AI libraries and frameworks.

3.2 Python Syntax and Structure

Python syntax is like grammar for this programming language. Syntax refers to the set of rules that defines how to write and organize code

Hello World Example

```
print("Hello, AI World!")
```

This simple command outputs text to the console and represents the starting point for all Python learners.

3.3 Variables, Data Types, and Expressions

In Python, a variable is simply a name that stores a value. Think of it like a label on a box. Unlike some other languages, you don't need to declare a variable's type explicitly in Python. Based on the value assigned, Python will dynamically determine the type.

Python Example:

```
x = 10          # integer
name = "AI"     # string
pi = 3.14       # float
is_ready = True   # Boolean
```

Common Data Types:

The common data types you'll use are:

Data Type	Description	Example
int	Whole numbers	42
float	Decimal numbers	3.14
str	Text strings	"Neural Net"
bool	Boolean values (True/False)	True
list	Ordered, mutable collection	[1, 2, 3]
tuple	Ordered, immutable collection	(1, 2, 3)
dict	Key-value pairs	{"x": 1, "y":2}

Operators and Expressions:

Python supports various operators for arithmetic, comparison, and logical operations.

Arithmetic operators:

```
a = 10
b = 3
print(a + b)    # 13
print(a - b)    # 7
print(a * b)    # 30
print(a / b)    # 3.333...
print(a % b)    # 1
```

Comparison operators:

```
print(a > b)    # True
print(a == b)   # False
```

Logical operators:

```
print(a > 5 and b < 5)   # True
print(a > 5 or b > 10)   # True
```

3.4 Python Data Structures

Python offers powerful **data structures** for handling collections of values.

Lists:

Lists are ordered collections of items.

```
numbers = [10, 20, 30, 40]
print(numbers[0])    # 10

numbers.append(50)
print(numbers)       # [10, 20, 30, 40, 50]
```

Dictionaries:

Dictionaries store data as key-value pairs.

```
student = {"name": "Alice", "age": 22, "score": 95}
print(student["name"])  # Alice
student["score"] = 98   # update value
```

Tuples:

Tuples are like lists, but immutable (cannot be changed).

```
point = (5, 10)
print(point[0])  # 5
```

Sets:

Sets are unordered collections of unique items.

```
unique_nums = {1, 2, 3, 3, 4}
print(unique_nums)  # {1, 2, 3, 4}
```

3.5 Conditional Statements and Loops

Conditional Statements:

Control flow structures allow your program to make decisions.

```
score = 85

if score >= 90:
   print("Excellent")
elif score >= 75:
   print("Good")
else:
   print("Keep practicing")
```

Loops:

Loops are essential for iterating over datasets or repeating tasks.

For Loop

For Loop is used to iterate over a sequence such as a list, tuple, string or range. It allows you to execute a block of code repeatedly, once for each item in the sequence.

```
for i in range(5):
    print(i)
```

While Loop

While loop is used to execute a block of statements repeatedly until a given condition is satisfied.

```
count = 0
while count < 3:
    print("AI is fun!")
    count += 1
```

3.6 Functions and Modules

Functions:

Functions let you organize reusable blocks of code. Python Functions are a block of statements that does a specific task.

```
def greet(name):
    return f"Hello, {name}!"

print(greet("AI Enthusiast"))
```

Modules:

Modules are Python files with reusable functions. You can import built-in or external ones.

```
import math
print(math.sqrt(16))  # 4.0
```

You can also create your own module (e.g. utils.py) and import it.

In AI, we'll import libraries (modules) like **NumPy, Pandas, TensorFlow** to handle complex tasks.

3.7 Python Coding Best Practices

As you begin writing Python code for AI development, following good coding practices becomes just as important as understanding the language itself. Clean, well-structured code is easier to read, debug, and extend—especially when working with data pipelines, machine learning models, and larger projects.

Using meaningful variable and function names helps make your code self-explanatory. Instead of short or ambiguous names, clear naming improves readability and reduces mistakes. Organizing code into small, reusable functions also makes it easier to test and modify individual components without breaking the entire program.

Consistency is another key practice. Following common Python conventions, such as indentation, spacing, and formatting, makes your code easier for others (and your future self) to understand. As AI projects grow in complexity, these habits will save time and prevent errors.

Developing good coding practices early will help you transition smoothly into working with AI libraries, collaborative projects, and real-world applications.

3.7.1 Practice Exercises in Jupyter Notebook

In Jupyter, each code cell can be executed individually, making it easy to test and iterate.

Example Workflow:

1. Create a new notebook in Jupyter.
2. Add code cells for each Python concept covered above.
3. Run each cell and observe the output immediately.

3.7.2 Summary

In this chapter, we explored Python basics crucial for AI development:

- ✓ Variables, data types, and operators
- ✓ Control flow (if-else, loops)
- ✓ Functions and data structures
- ✓ Importing and using libraries
- ✓ Writing clean, readable code

These foundational skills will prepare you for more advanced topics like **NumPy arrays and Pandas DataFrames**, which we will cover in the next chapter.

Chapter 4:
Working with NumPy, Pandas, Matplotlib for AI

4.1 Introduction

In the world of artificial intelligence, **data is everything**. Whether you're training a machine learning model, analyzing user behavior, or building predictive systems, you need to work with data—often in massive volumes. But raw data is rarely clean, structured, or immediately useful. That's why every AI practitioner must be skilled in **data manipulation**, **numerical computation**, and **visualization**.

This chapter introduces three of the most powerful and widely used Python libraries in the AI developer's toolkit:

- **NumPy** (Numerical Python): The foundation for numerical computing in Python. It enables fast operations on large arrays and matrices, which are essential for everything from linear algebra to deep learning.
- **Pandas**: A data analysis and manipulation library that allows you to work efficiently with structured data like tables (DataFrames). It makes tasks like data cleaning, filtering, and summarizing simple and intuitive.
- **Matplotlib**: A versatile visualization library for creating static, animated, and interactive plots. It helps you explore data, understand patterns, and communicate results clearly.

Together, these tools allow you to:

- Load and clean datasets
- Perform efficient numerical operations
- Analyze and summarize data
- Visualize data to uncover hidden patterns or trends

Before diving into machine learning and deep learning, it's critical to become comfortable with handling data effectively. Think of NumPy, Pandas, and Matplotlib as your **data science power trio**—tools you'll return to again and again throughout your AI journey.

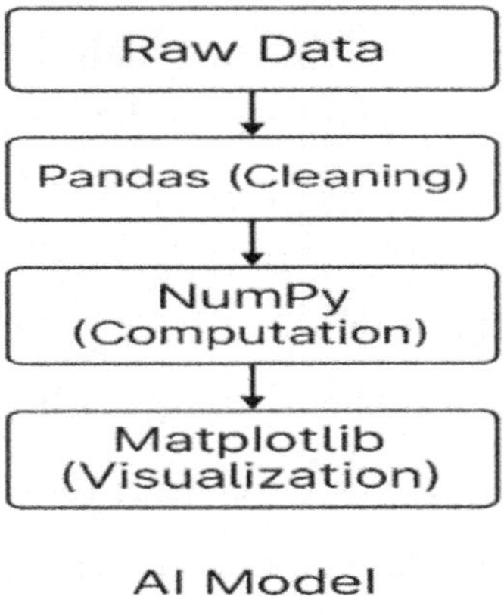

4.2 NumPy for Numerical Computing

When working with AI models, especially those involving large datasets or numerical operations like matrix multiplication, **performance matters**. Python's built-in lists are flexible but not optimized for numerical computing. That's where **NumPy** comes in.

What Is NumPy?

NumPy (Numerical Python) is a fundamental package for numerical computing with Python. It provides:

- **N-Dimensional Arrays:** A powerful **multi-dimensional array** object (ndarray)
- **High Performance Arrays**: Arrays are stored in contiguous memory locations, enabling faster computations than Python lists.
- **Broadcasting:** This allows element-wise computations between arrays of different shapes
- **Vectorization:** Apply operations directly on entire arrays which eliminates the need for explicit Python loops.
- **Linear algebra:** Tools for linear algebra, random number generation, and more.

NumPy arrays are **faster** and **more memory-efficient** than traditional Python lists, making them ideal for AI applications where performance is crucial.

Creating NumPy Arrays:

Let's start by importing NumPy and creating a simple array:

```
import numpy as np

# Creating a 1D array
a = np.array([1, 2, 3])
print(a)

# Creating a 2D array
b = np.array([[1, 2, 3], [4, 5, 6]])
print(b)
```

You can also create arrays filled with zeros, ones, or random numbers:

```
np.zeros((2, 3))       # 2x3 array of zeros
np.ones((3, 3))        # 3x3 array of ones
np.random.rand(2, 2) # 2x2 array with random values
```

Array Operations and Broadcasting:

NumPy allows for element-wise arithmetic and supports **broadcasting**, which enables operations between arrays of different shapes.

```
a = np.array([1, 2, 3])
b = np.array([4, 5, 6])

print(a + b)    # [5 7 9]
print(a * b)    # [4 10 18]

# Broadcasting:
a = np.array([[1], [2], [3]])    # 3x1 array
b = np.array([10, 20, 30])       # 1D array

print(a + b)
```

Indexing, Slicing, and Reshaping:

Like Python lists, you can index and slice NumPy arrays. Plus, you can reshape them easily.

```
a = np.array([[1, 2, 3], [4, 5, 6]])

print(a[0, 1]) # Access element at row 0, column 1 → 2
print(a[:, 1]) # Get the second column → [2 5]
print(a[1, :]) # Get the second row → [4 5 6]

# Reshape a 1D array into a 2x3 matrix
b = np.arange(6).reshape(2, 3)
print(b)
```

Useful NumPy Functions for AI

These functions are commonly used in AI workflows:

```
data = np.array([[1, 2, 3], [4, 5, 6]])

np.mean(data)          # Mean of all elements
np.std(data)           # Standard deviation
np.sum(data, axis=0) # Column-wise sum
np.dot(a, b)           # Matrix multiplication
```

4.3 Pandas for Data Manipulation

In AI and data science, you will frequently work with **structured data**—data organized in rows and columns, like a spreadsheet or a database table. While NumPy is great for raw numerical arrays, it isn't designed for labeled, tabular datasets. That's where **Pandas** shines.

What Is Pandas?

Pandas is a Python library for data analysis and manipulation. It provides two key data structures:

- **Series** – A one-dimensional labeled array
- **DataFrame** – A two-dimensional labeled table

With Pandas, you can:

- Load data from CSV, Excel, SQL, JSON, and more
- Clean, filter, and transform datasets
- Handle missing data
- Perform aggregations and group-based operations

Creating Pandas Data Structures:

```
import pandas as pd

# Creating a Series
s = pd.Series([10, 20, 30], index=["a", "b", "c"])
print(s)

# Creating a DataFrame
data = {
   "Name": ["Alice", "Bob", "Charlie"],
   "Score": [85, 90, 78],
   "Passed": [True, True, False]
}
df = pd.DataFrame(data)
print(df)
```

Example Output:

Name	Score	Passed
Alice	85	True
Bob	90	True
Charlie	78	False

Selecting and Filtering Data:

```
# Selecting a single column
print(df["Name"])

# Selecting multiple columns
print(df[["Name", "Score"]])

# Filtering rows
print(df[df["Score"] > 80])
```

Handling Missing Data:

```
# Checking for missing values
print(df.isnull().sum())

# Filling missing values
df["Score"] = df["Score"].fillna(df["Score"].mean())

# Dropping missing values
df = df.dropna()
```

Grouping and Aggregation:

```
# Grouping by a column and calculating the mean
grouped = df.groupby("Passed")["Score"].mean()
print(grouped)
```

Reading and Writing Data:

```
# Reading from CSV
df = pd.read_csv("data.csv")

# Writing to CSV
df.to_csv("output.csv", index=False)

# Reading from Excel
df = pd.read_excel("data.xlsx")
```

4.4 Matplotlib for Data Visualization

Visualizing data is how you **explore patterns, debug assumptions**, and **communicate results**. In Python, **Matplotlib** is the foundational plotting library that everything else builds on. Even high-level libraries (like pandas plotting and Seaborn) sit on top of Matplotlib.

What Is Matplotlib?

Matplotlib is a flexible library for creating static, animated, and interactive plots. You'll use it to:

- Inspect distributions (histograms)
- Compare categories (bar charts)
- Explore relationships (scatter plots)
- Track values over time (line charts)

Basic Plot Anatomy:

```
import matplotlib.pyplot as plt
# Minimal line plot
x = [0, 1, 2, 3, 4]
y = [0, 1, 4, 9, 16]

plt.plot(x, y, marker="o")
plt.title("Simple Line Plot")
plt.xlabel("x")
plt.ylabel("y")
plt.grid(True)
plt.show()
```

Key parts:

- plt.plot(...) draws the series.
- plt.title, plt.xlabel, plt.ylabel add context.
- plt.grid(True) helps readability.
- plt.show() renders the figure (important in scripts).

Example Output:

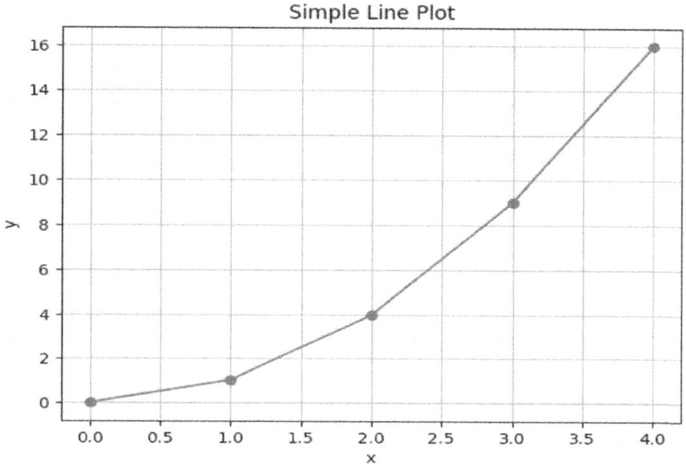

Common Plot Types:

1) Line Plot (trends over an index or time)

```
days = [1, 2, 3, 4, 5, 6, 7]
visitors = [120, 135, 150, 160, 145, 170, 190]

plt.plot(days, visitors, marker="o")
plt.title("Daily Visitors (Last 7 Days)")
plt.xlabel("Day")
plt.ylabel("Visitors")
plt.show()
```

2) Histogram (distribution)

```
import numpy as np
scores = np.random.normal(loc=75, scale=10, size=300)
plt.hist(scores, bins=20)
plt.title("Score Distribution")
plt.xlabel("Score")
plt.ylabel("Frequency")
plt.show()
```

3) Bar Chart (category comparisons)

```
languages = ["Python", "Java", "C++", "JavaScript"]
counts = [58, 39, 25, 46]
plt.bar(languages, counts)
plt.title("Course Enrollments by Language")
plt.xlabel("Language")
plt.ylabel("Enrollments")
plt.show()
```

Example Output:

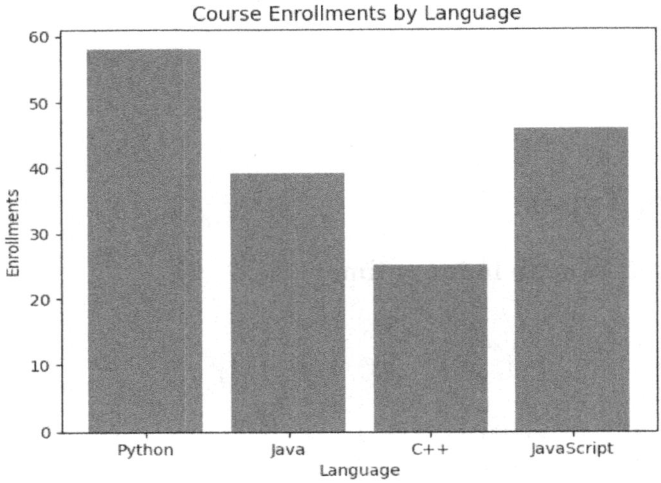

4) Scatter Plot (relationships/correlation)

```
study_hours = [2, 3, 4, 5, 7, 8, 10]
exam_scores = [60, 62, 68, 72, 80, 86, 92]
plt.scatter(study_hours, exam_scores)
plt.title("Study Hours vs Exam Score")
plt.xlabel("Study Hours")
plt.ylabel("Exam Score")
plt.show()
```

Using Pandas with Matplotlib:

Pandas integrates tightly with Matplotlib via .plot(...) for quick charts:

```
import pandas as pd

df = pd.DataFrame({
    "month": ["Jan", "Feb", "Mar", "Apr", "May"],
    "users": [120, 150, 180, 200, 260],
    "revenue": [900, 1100, 1500, 1600, 2100]
})

# Line from DataFrame
df.plot(x="month", y="users", marker="o", title="Active Users")
plt.xlabel("Month")
plt.ylabel("Users")
plt.grid(True)
plt.show()
```

Example Output:

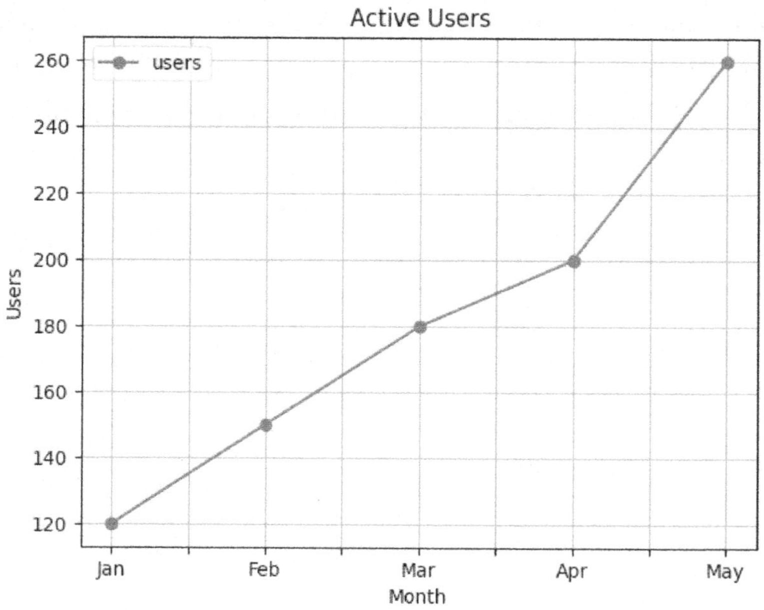

4.5 Summary

In this chapter, you learned how to work with data using three essential Python libraries: NumPy, Pandas, and Matplotlib. These tools form the foundation of most AI and data science workflows and are used extensively throughout machine learning and deep learning projects.

You started by using NumPy for numerical operations and array-based computations, which are critical for efficient data processing. You then explored Pandas to load, manipulate, and analyze structured datasets, making it easier to clean data and extract meaningful insights. Finally, you used Matplotlib to visualize data, helping you understand patterns, trends, and relationships before applying AI models.

By mastering these tools, you now have the skills needed to prepare and explore datasets effectively. This ability to understand data visually and numerically is a crucial step before building machine learning models, which you will begin exploring in the next part of this book.

Part II – Artificial Intelligence & Machine Learning

Chapter 5:
What Is Artificial Intelligence?

5.1 Introduction

Artificial Intelligence (AI) is one of the most transformative technologies of our time. At its core, AI refers to the ability of machines to **simulate human intelligence**—learning from data, reasoning, adapting, and making decisions. Unlike traditional software, which follows fixed instructions, AI systems can improve their performance over time by **learning from experience**.

Although the idea of intelligent machines dates back to the 1950s, recent advances in data availability, computing power, and algorithmic innovation have made modern AI practical and widely accessible. Today, AI powers many of the technologies we interact with every day, including:

- Virtual assistants such as Siri, Alexa, and Google Assistant
- Recommendation systems used by streaming and e-commerce platforms
- Fraud detection systems in banking and finance
- Autonomous vehicles and intelligent navigation systems

In the context of this book, AI is not treated as an abstract or theoretical concept. Instead, it is approached as a **practical set of tools and techniques** that you will learn to apply using Python. By the end of this journey, you will understand how AI systems work and how to build real-world AI applications yourself.

Before diving deeper, it is important to clarify a common source of confusion—the difference between Artificial Intelligence, Machine Learning, and Deep Learning.

5.2 AI vs Machine Learning vs Deep Learning

The terms **Artificial Intelligence (AI), Machine Learning (ML)**, and **Deep Learning (DL)** are often used interchangeably, but they represent different concepts. A useful way to understand them is as **nested layers**, where each builds upon the previous one.

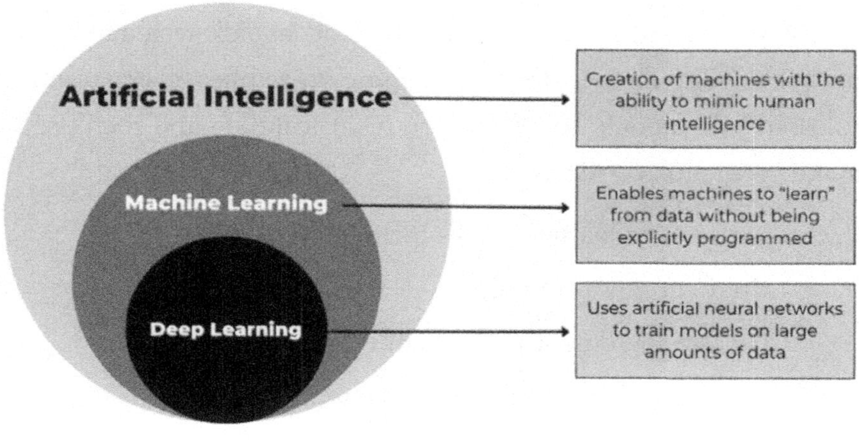

Artificial Intelligence (AI):

AI is the **broad field** focused on creating machines capable of performing tasks that typically require **human intelligence**. These tasks include reasoning, problem-solving, perception, and language understanding.

Examples of AI systems include:

- Playing strategic games such as chess (Deep Blue by IBM)
- Understanding and generating human language (ChatGPT)
- Recognizing faces in images
- Planning optimal routes for delivery or navigation

AI systems do not always rely on learning from data. They can also use:

- Rule-based systems
- Search and optimization algorithms
- Expert systems

Machine Learning (ML):

Machine Learning is a **subset of AI** that enables systems to **learn patterns from data** instead of relying on explicitly programmed rules. In ML, models are trained on historical data and then used to make predictions or decisions.

Common machine learning tasks include:

- Predicting house prices
- Classifying emails as spam or not spam
- Recommending products or content

Deep Learning (DL):

Deep Learning is a **subset of ML** that uses **artificial neural networks**—inspired by the human brain—to automatically learn complex patterns. The "deep" refers to having many layers in the network, allowing the model to extract higher-level features at each stage.

Deep Learning is widely used in:

- Image and video recognition
- Speech recognition
- Language translation
- Generative AI systems for text and images

Popular deep learning architectures include Convolutional Neural Networks (CNNs) for images and Transformer-based models for text and sequences.

Key Takeaway:

- **AI** is the overall goal: creating intelligent systems
- **ML** is one approach to achieving AI by learning from data
- **DL** is a powerful ML technique using multi-layer neural networks

5.3 Real-World Applications of AI

Artificial Intelligence is no longer confined to research labs—it is deeply embedded in modern industries and everyday applications.

Healthcare:

- AI supports medical diagnosis, imaging analysis, and patient risk prediction.
- *Impact:* Faster diagnoses, personalized treatments, and improved patient outcomes.

Finance:

- AI is used for fraud detection, algorithmic trading, and customer support automation.
- *Impact:* Increased security and smarter financial decision-making.

Transportation:

- Autonomous vehicles and intelligent traffic systems rely on AI for navigation and safety.
- *Impact:* Safer roads, reduced congestion, and efficient logistics.

Retail and E-Commerce:

- AI personalizes shopping experiences, optimizes pricing, and manages inventory.
- *Impact:* Better customer experiences and increased sales.

Natural Language Processing and Generative AI:

- AI enables machines to understand and generate human language, powering chatbots, assistants, and content-generation tools.
- *Impact:* Improved communication, productivity, and automation.

As AI continues to evolve, its applications will expand further into areas such as education, agriculture, energy, and scientific research.

5.4 The AI Application Workflow

No matter the application—whether it's predicting house prices, translating languages, or recognizing faces—AI development generally follows a **structured workflow**. Understanding this process helps clarify how AI solutions are built from start to finish.

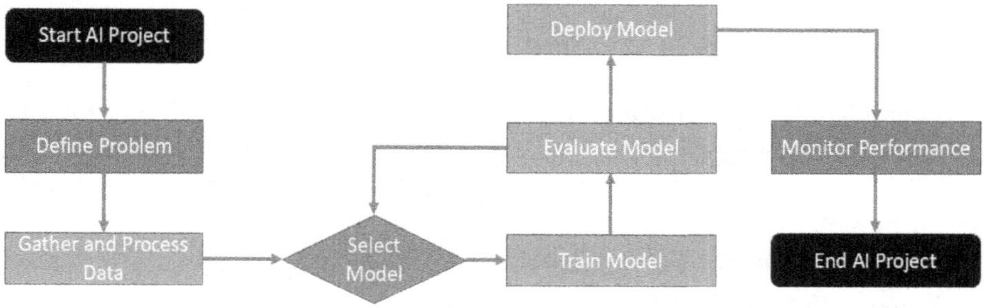

Step 1: Problem Definition:

Before starting an AI project, clearly define the problem:

- What problem you are solving
- What kind of output you need
- How success will be measured

Example: Predict whether a customer will make a purchase within 30 days.

Step 2: Data Collection:

AI thrives on data. Gather relevant data from sources such as:

- Existing databases
- APIs, Web scraping
- Sensors, IoT devices, Open datasets

Example: Collect historical customer interactions from an e-commerce database.

Step 3: Data Preprocessing & Cleaning:

Raw data is often messy—full of missing values, inconsistencies, and irrelevant features. Prepare raw data by:

- Handle missing values (imputation or removal)
- Remove duplicates or inconsistencies,
- Encode categorical data
- Normalize or standardize numerical values

Example: Fill missing purchase dates with "no purchase" and encode product categories as numbers.

Step 4: Model Selection:

Choose an appropriate ML algorithm based on the problem type such as:

- Regression models for predicting numbers
- Classification models for predicting categories
- Clustering for grouping data without labels
- Neural networks for complex, non-linear problems

Example: Use Logistic Regression to classify customers as likely/not likely to purchase.

Step 5: Training the Model:

Train the model using historical data so it can learn patterns. During training:

- Split data into **training** and **validation** sets
- optimize parameters and reduce errors

Step 6: Evaluation:

Test the model on unseen data to assess performance. Assess model performance using suitable metrics and compare results against baselines

Step 7: Deployment:

Integrate the trained model into a real-world system such as a web application or API.

Step 8: Continuous Improvement:

AI isn't "train once and forget." It's a cycle. Monitor performance, collect new data, retrain models, and adapt to changing conditions.

This workflow forms the backbone of modern AI development and will be revisited throughout the book.

5.5 Summary

This chapter defined **Artificial Intelligence** as the broad effort to build machines with human-like intelligence, while clarifying the relationship between its key subsets:

- **Machine Learning (ML):** Teaching systems to recognize patterns in data.
- **Deep Learning (DL):** Using multi-layered neural networks for complex tasks like vision and language.

We explored **real-world applications** across various industries and introduced the **AI Workflow**, the standard step-by-step process for developing and deploying models. Next, we will dive into learning paradigms to begin **building your first ML model**.

Chapter 6: Introduction to Machine Learning

Machine Learning (ML) is at the heart of today's artificial intelligence revolution. From recommendation systems to self-driving cars, ML enables computers to discover patterns and make predictions from data — without being explicitly programmed for every task.

In this chapter, you'll learn the foundations of machine learning, explore its main types, understand core concepts, get an overview of popular algorithms, and finally build your very first ML model in Python using **scikit-learn**.

6.1 What Is Machine Learning?

Machine Learning is a subset of Artificial Intelligence that focuses on creating systems that can **learn from data**. Instead of manually coding every rule, you provide examples and let the algorithm infer the underlying relationships.

Example: A traditional spam filter might rely on hard-coded keywords. A machine-learning spam filter is trained on thousands of emails labeled "spam" or "not spam," and it automatically learns which features (e.g., sender address, specific phrases) indicate spam.

Machine learning is used everywhere:

- Netflix and Spotify recommendations
- Fraud detection in banking
- Medical diagnosis from images
- Autonomous vehicles
- Natural language translation

The key takeaway: ML is about **experience-based improvement** – the more relevant data, the better a model can generalize to new situations.

6.2 Types of Machine Learning

ML can be broadly categorized into three main types:

1. Supervised Learning:

- Learns from **labeled data** (inputs paired with correct outputs).
- Goal: predict an outcome for new, unseen data.
- Tasks:
    - **Regression** – predicting continuous values (e.g., house prices).
    - **Classification** – predicting categories (e.g., "spam" vs. "not spam").

2. Unsupervised Learning:

- Works with **unlabeled data**, discovering hidden patterns.
- Tasks:
    - **Clustering** – grouping similar data (e.g., customer segmentation).
    - **Dimensionality reduction** – simplifying data while retaining structure (e.g., PCA).

3. Reinforcement Learning:

- An agent (AI) learns by interacting with an environment and receiving **rewards or penalties**.
- Examples: game-playing AIs, robotics, autonomous driving.

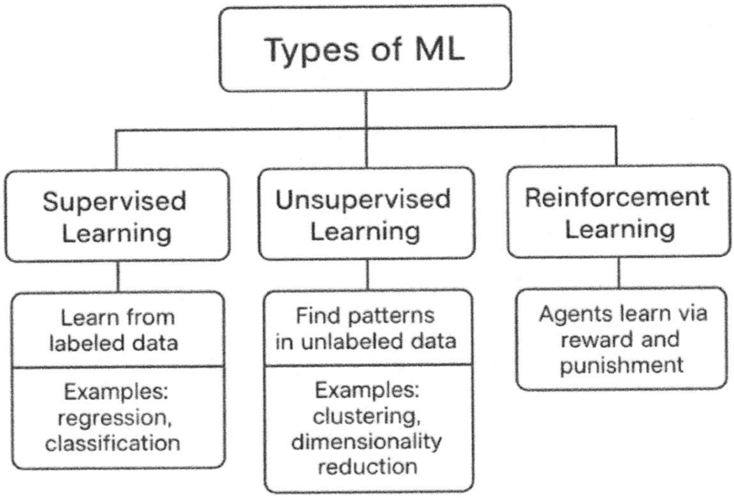

6.3 Core Machine Learning Concepts

Before you can train a model, it's crucial to understand the basic building blocks:

- **Features (X):** Input variables describing each observation (e.g., square footage, number of bedrooms).
- **Label/Target (y):** The value you want to predict (e.g., house price).
- **Training Data:** A dataset used to teach the algorithm how features relate to labels.
- **Testing Data:** A separate dataset used to evaluate how well the model generalizes.

Overfitting vs. Underfitting:

- **Overfitting:** The model memorizes training data too closely and fails to generalize.
- **Underfitting:** The model is too simple to capture important patterns.

☑ Always aim for a balance: a model that performs well on both training and testing data.

6.4 Popular Machine Learning Algorithms

Machine learning algorithms come in many flavors. Here's a high-level overview:

Category	Algorithm and Use Case
Regression	Linear Regression, Ridge/Lasso **Use Case:** Predicting prices, trends
Classification	Logistic Regression, Decision Trees, Random Forests, Support Vector Machines, k-NN **Use case:** Email spam detection, medical diagnosis
Clustering	k-Means, Hierarchical Clustering **Use Case:** Customer segmentation
Dimensionality Reduction	PCA, t-SNE **Use Case**: Data visualization, noise reduction
Ensemble Methods	Gradient Boosting, XGBoost **Use Case:** Improving accuracy via combined models
Neural Networks	Deep Learning models **Use Case:** Image recognition, NLP

You don't need to master them all immediately — focus on understanding the concepts, then explore algorithms as needed.

6.5 Introduction to scikit-learn

scikit-learn is one of the most widely used Python libraries for machine learning. It provides simple, consistent tools for building, training, and evaluating machine learning models, making it an ideal choice for beginners as well as professionals.

Rather than implementing algorithms from scratch, scikit-learn allows you to focus on **applying machine learning concepts** to real data. It includes ready-to-use implementations of common algorithms such as linear regression, decision trees, and classification models, along with utilities for data preprocessing and model evaluation.

A typical machine learning workflow in scikit-learn follows a clear and intuitive pattern:

1. **Prepare the data** – Load the dataset and organize features and labels.
2. **Split the data** – Separate data into training and testing sets.
3. **Choose a model** – Select an appropriate algorithm for the problem.
4. **Train the model** – Fit the model to the training data.
5. **Evaluate performance** – Measure how well the model performs on unseen data.

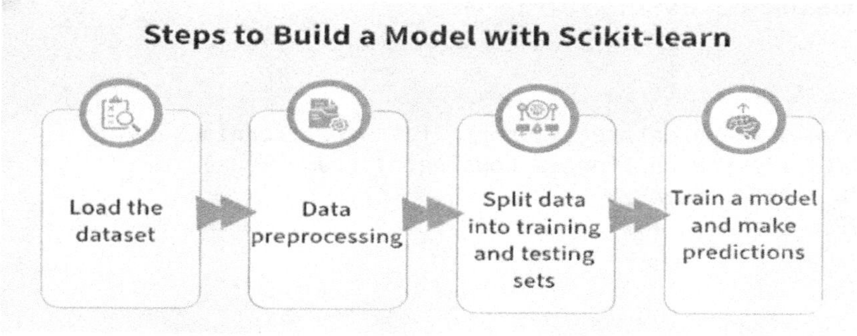

6.6 Hands-On: Building Your First Machine Learning Model

In this hands-on exercise, we'll build a simple **Linear Regression** model using **scikit-learn**. Linear Regression predicts a continuous numeric value for example, estimating house prices.

Here, our goal is to **illustrate the complete machine-learning workflow**:

loading data → preparing features → training a model → evaluating results.

We'll explore the theory and details of Linear Regression in **Chapter 7: Supervised Learning with Python**.

Step 1: Import Libraries

```
import pandas as pd
from sklearn.model_selection import train_test_split
from sklearn.linear_model import LinearRegression
from sklearn.metrics import mean_squared_error, r2_score
```

Step 2: Load a Dataset

For simplicity, we'll use the built-in **California housing** dataset.

```
from sklearn.datasets import  fetch_california_housing
data = fetch_california_housing(as_frame=True)
df = data.frame
df.head()
```

	MedInc	HouseAge	AveRooms	AveBedrms	Population	AveOccup	Latitude	Longitude	MedHouseVal
0	8.3252	41.0	6.984127	1.023810	322.0	2.555556	37.88	-122.23	4.526
1	8.3014	21.0	6.238137	0.971880	2401.0	2.109842	37.86	-122.22	3.585
2	7.2574	52.0	8.288136	1.073446	496.0	2.802260	37.85	-122.24	3.521
3	5.6431	52.0	5.817352	1.073059	558.0	2.547945	37.85	-122.25	3.413
4	3.8462	52.0	6.281853	1.081081	565.0	2.181467	37.85	-122.25	3.422

Step 3: Prepare Features and Labels

```
X = df.drop(columns=['MedHouseVal'])  # Features
y = df['MedHouseVal']                 # Target
```

Step 4: Split into Training and Testing Sets

```
X_train, X_test, y_train, y_test = train_test_split(
    X, y, test_size=0.2, random_state=42)
```

Step 5: Train the Model

```
model = LinearRegression()
model.fit(X_train, y_train)
```

Step 6: Make Predictions

```
y_pred = model.predict(X_test)
```

Step 7: Evaluate Performance

```
mse = mean_squared_error(y_test, y_pred)
r2 = r2_score(y_test, y_pred)

print("Mean Squared Error:", mse)
print("R² Score:", r2)
```

Step 8: Visualize Results

```
import matplotlib.pyplot as plt

plt.scatter(y_test, y_pred, alpha=0.5)
plt.xlabel("Actual Prices")
plt.ylabel("Predicted Prices")
plt.title("Actual vs Predicted House Prices")
plt.show()
```

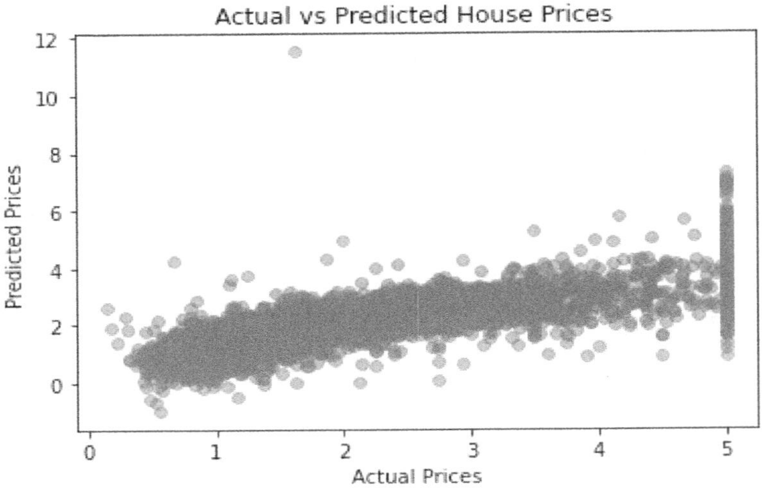

6.7 Summary

In this chapter, you:

- ✓ Discovered what machine learning is and its primary types.
- ✓ Learned about features, labels, training/testing, and model performance.
- ✓ Explored popular ML algorithms.
- ✓ Used scikit-learn to build and evaluate a simple **Linear Regression** model.

You now have a solid foundation to dive deeper into other algorithms and more advanced ML concepts in the coming chapters.

Chapter 7:
Supervised Learning with Python

In the previous chapter, we explored the fundamentals of machine learning - understanding how machines learn from data, the overall workflow of model building, and the role of Python libraries like Scikit-learn in simplifying the process. Now, we're ready to dive deeper into one of the most important branches of machine learning: Supervised Learning.

7.1 What Is Supervised Learning?

Supervised learning is the foundational machine learning technique where a model learns from labelled data, meaning every input has a corresponding correct output. During training, it repeatedly makes predictions, calculates the error against the true labels, and adjusts its internal parameters to minimize this discrepancy. The main goal is to make accurate predictions on new, unseen data. For example, a model trained on images of handwritten digits can recognise new digits it has never seen before.

Types of Supervised Learning:

Supervised learning problems fall into two main categories based on the type of output the model predicts.

- **Regression:** involves predicting **continuous numeric values,** where outputs can take any value within a range. Regression models are used to estimate quantities or trends, such as predicting house prices, forecasting sales, or estimating temperatures.

- **Classification:** involves predicting **discrete categories or labels**. The model assigns inputs to predefined classes, such as identifying spam emails, detecting fraudulent transactions, or recognizing objects in images.

The choice between regression and classification depends on the **nature of the target variable**. If the output is a number, the problem is regression; if the output represents a category, it is classification. This distinction is fundamental when selecting algorithms and evaluation methods.

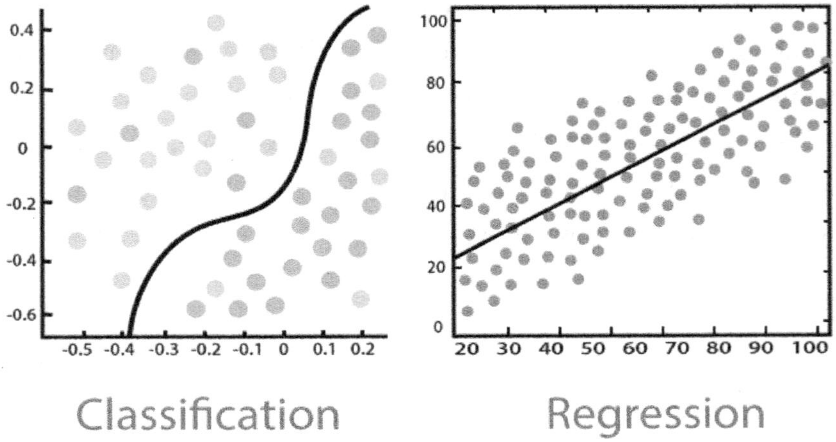

7.2 How Supervised Learning Works

While training the model, data is usually split in the ratio of 80:20 i.e. 80% as training data and the rest as testing data. In training data, we feed input as well as output for 80% of data. The model learns from training data only.

Every supervised learning project follows a structured process:

1. **Data Collection** – Gather relevant, labeled data.
2. **Data Preparation** – Clean and preprocess the data by handling missing values, encoding categorical variables, and normalizing numerical features.
3. **Splitting Data** – Divide the dataset into a **training set** and a **test set**. The model learns from the training data and is evaluated on the test data.
4. **Training the Model** – Choose an algorithm and feed the training data into it.
5. **Evaluating the Model** – Measure performance using metrics such as accuracy, mean absolute error, or R^2 score.
6. **Improving the Model** – Adjust parameters, try different algorithms, or gather more data to improve performance.

This workflow helps ensure that your model not only performs well on the data it has seen but also generalizes effectively to new data.

The Supervised Learning Workflow

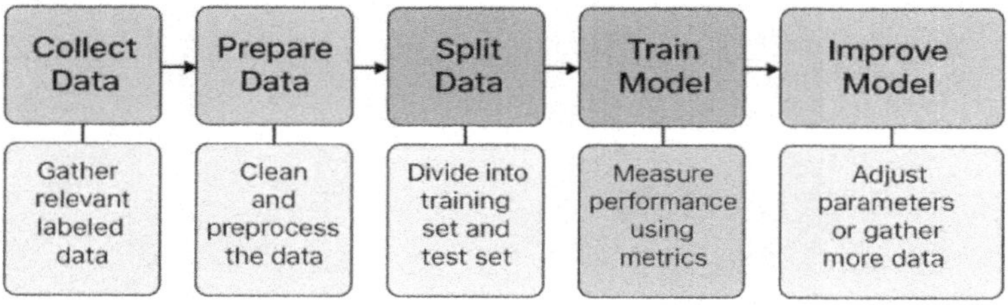

7.3 Regression: Predicting Continuous Values

Regression is used when the target variable is a continuous numeric value. For example, predicting house prices based on the size of the house, number of bedrooms, or location.

7.3.1 Linear Regression:

Linear regression is one of the simplest forms of regression used for predicting continuous values based on input features.

- Linear regression is a relationship between the **input features** (independent variables) and the **target outcome** (dependent variable).
- The goal is to find the best-fitting **straight line** that represents the data. This line, known as the regression line, allows us to predict a continuous outcome (e.g., house prices, temperature).
- Essentially, linear regression models the relationship between a dependent variable (the outcome you want to predict) and one or more independent variables (the input features you use for prediction) by finding the best-fitting straight line through a set of data points.
- The equation for a simple linear regression line is defined as:

  $y = m\,x + c$

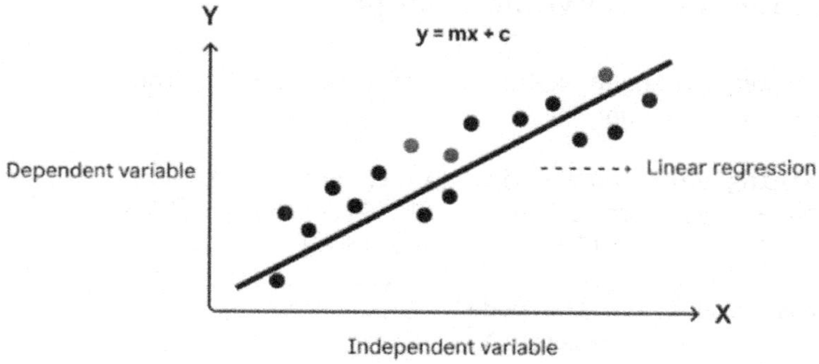

Where:

- y is the predicted output (e.g., price)
- x is the input feature (e.g., size)
- m is the slope of the line
- c is the intercept (where the line crosses the y-axis)
- The goal of Linear Regression is to find the best-fitting line that represents this data, which means finding the optimal values for m and c.

Linear regression is fast, interpretable, and serves as an excellent starting.

Linear Regression Python Example:

```
from sklearn.linear_model import LinearRegression
import numpy as np

# Training data: house size (X) vs price (y)
X = np.array([[800], [1000], [1200], [1500], [1800]])
y = np.array([90, 110, 130, 150, 180])

# Create and train the model
model = LinearRegression()
model.fit(X, y)

# Predict price for a new house size
pred = model.predict([[1600]])

# Display result
print('Predicted price for 1600 sqft:', round(pred[0]))
```

Example Output:

```
Predicted price for 1600 sqft: 162
```

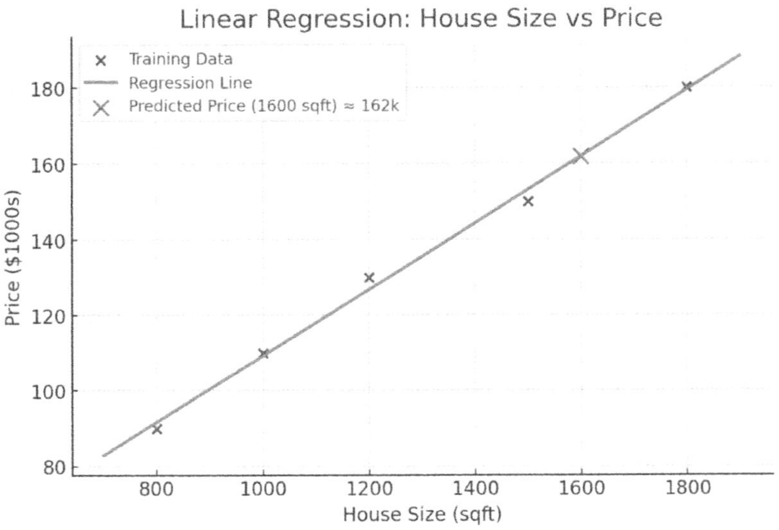

7.4 Classification: Predicting Categories

Classification is used when the output variable represents categories or classes rather than numeric values. Examples include:

- Determining whether an email is spam or not.
- Predicting whether a patient has diabetes.
- Identifying the species of a flower from petal and sepal measurements.

7.4.1 Logistic Regression

Despite its name, **Logistic Regression** is a **classification** algorithm. It estimates the probability that an observation belongs to a certain class. The output of logistic regression is a probability value between 0 and 1, which is then converted into a class label using a threshold (commonly 0.5).

For instance, if a model predicts that a student has a **0.8 probability of passing**, it classifies the student as "Pass." Logistic regression uses a **sigmoid function** to map input values into this probability range.

Logistic Regression Python Example:

```
from sklearn.linear_model import LogisticRegression
import numpy as np

# Training data: hours studied vs exam result(1=Pass,0=Fail)
X = np.array([[1], [2], [3], [4], [5], [6]])
y = np.array([0, 0, 0, 1, 1, 1])

# Create and train the model
model = LogisticRegression()
model.fit(X, y)

# Predict whether a student who studied 4.5 hours passes
pred = model.predict([[4.5]])
prob = model.predict_proba([[4.5]])

# Display results
print("Predicted class (1=Pass):", int(pred[0]))
print("Probability of passing:", round(prob[0][1], 2))
```

Example Output:

```
Predicted class (1=Pass): 1
Probability of passing: 0.75
```

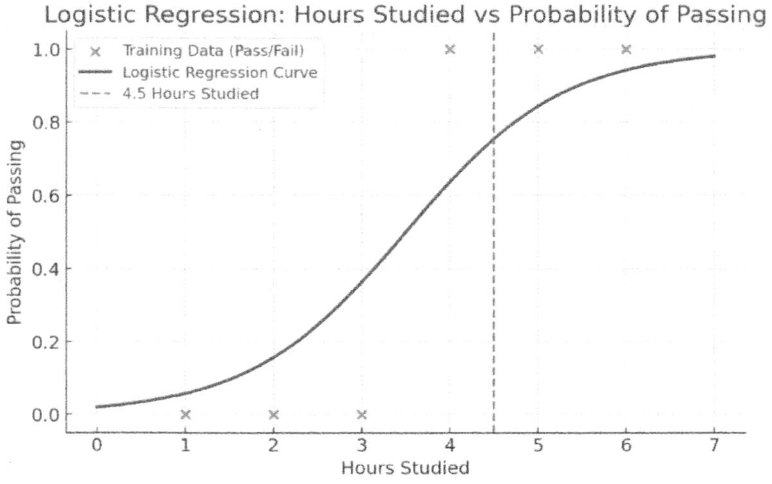

7.4.2 Decision Trees

A Decision Tree mimics human decision-making by splitting data into branches based on specific conditions. It reaches a prediction via "yes/no" questions; for example: **"Is it raining?"** or **"Is it windy?"**

Decision Trees Python Example:

```
from sklearn.tree import DecisionTreeClassifier

# Training data: [Rain, Windy] (1=Yes, 0=No)
X = [[0, 0], [0, 1], [1, 0], [1, 1]]
y = [1, 0, 0, 0]  # Play (1) only if not raining and not windy

# Create and train the decision tree
model = DecisionTreeClassifier(random_state=42)
model.fit(X, y)

# Predict for a new day: Rainy (1) and Not Windy (0)
pred = model.predict([[1, 0]])

# Display result. Play match if its not raining and not windy
print("Predicted class (1=Play, 0=No):", int(pred[0]))
```

Example Output:

```
Predicted class (1=Play, 0=No): 0
```

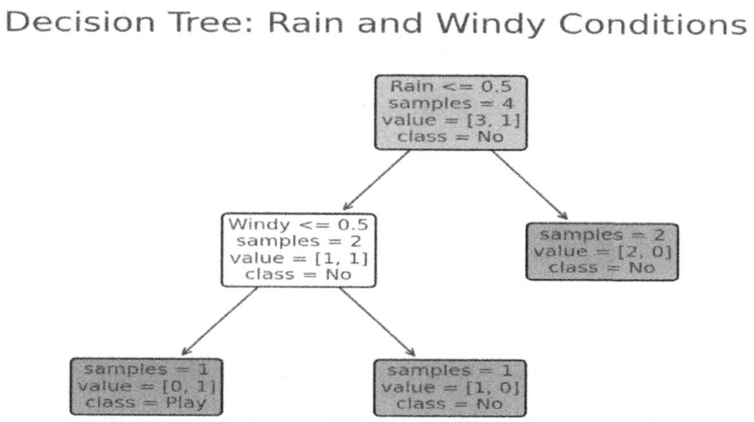

7.4.3 Random Forests

While a single **Decision Tree** is easy to understand, it can sometimes **overfit** learning too much from training data and performing poorly on new data.

A **Random Forest** solves this problem by combining **many Decision Trees** and averaging their predictions.

This technique is called an **ensemble method**, and it makes the model more accurate and stable

7.5 Evaluating Model Performance

When building machine learning models, it's important to understand how well they perform. **Evaluation metrics** help measure a model's effectiveness and guide you in improving it.

Regression Evaluation Metrics:

- **Mean Absolute Error (MAE):** The average of the absolute differences between predicted and actual values.
- **Mean Squared Error (MSE):** Similar to MAE, but gives *higher weight* to larger errors, making it more sensitive to outliers.
- **R^2 Score (Coefficient of Determination):** Indicates how much of the target variable's variability is explained by the model (1.0 means a perfect fit).

Classification Evaluation Metrics:

- **Accuracy:** The proportion of total predictions that are correct.
- **Precision:** The percentage of predicted positives that are actually positive.

- **Recall (Sensitivity):** The percentage of actual positives that were correctly identified.
- **F1 Score:** The harmonic mean of precision and recall — a balanced measure for imbalanced data.
- **Confusion Matrix:** A table that shows counts of true positives, false positives, true negatives, and false negatives, helping visualize where the model makes mistakes.

Evaluating your model with **multiple metrics** helps you understand not only *how often* it is right, but also *how and why* it might be wrong.

A hands-on example of these evaluation metrics is provided at the **end of this chapter**.

7.6 Comparing and Selecting Models

Different algorithms behave differently on the same data. For example, a Decision Tree might perform well on a small dataset but overfit when the dataset grows. To **fairly compare models**, we use **cross-validation**, a technique that splits the data into multiple subsets and tests the model on each.

The model's average performance across all folds provides a more reliable estimate of how it will perform on unseen data.

Cross-validation helps you:

- Compare multiple algorithms under the same conditions.
- Select the most suitable model for your task.
- Tune **hyperparameters** — special settings that control how a model learns (e.g., tree depth, learning rate, or number of estimators).

7.7 Saving and Using Trained Models

Once your model performs well, you can **save it for future use** instead of retraining it every time. Python provides the **joblib** and **pickle** libraries for this purpose.

For example, after training a classifier, you can save it as a file (model.pkl) and later reload it to make instant predictions:

```
import joblib
# Save model
joblib.dump(model, "model.pkl")

# Load model
loaded_model = joblib.load("model.pkl")
pred = loaded_model.predict([[1, 0]])
```

This capability is essential when **deploying machine learning systems** to production environments such as web applications, APIs, or cloud platforms.

7.8 Hands-On: Predicting House Prices using Supervised Learning

Dataset:

We'll use the **California Housing dataset** from sklearn, which includes information about housing districts in California:

- **Features:** median income, house age, average rooms, population, latitude, longitude, etc.
- **Target:** median house value (in $100,000s)

Project Goal:

Develop a **Linear Regression model** to predict median house prices using the dataset.We'll train the model and evaluate it.

Steps

1. Load the dataset using fetch_california_housing.
2. Split it into training and testing sets.
3. Train a **Linear Regression** model.
4. Evaluate model performance using **MAE**, **RMSE**, and **R^2**.
5. Predict the price for a new sample.

Python Code:

```
# Hands-on Project: Predicting California House Prices
from sklearn.datasets import fetch_california_housing
from sklearn.model_selection import train_test_split
from sklearn.linear_model import LinearRegression
from sklearn.metrics import mean_absolute_error
from sklearn.metrics import mean_squared_error, r2_score
import pandas as pd

# Step 1: Load dataset
data = fetch_california_housing(as_frame=True)
X, y = data.data, data.target  # target in $100,000s

# Step 2: Split into training and testing sets
X_train, X_test, y_train, y_test = train_test_split(
    X, y, test_size=0.2, random_state=42
)

# Step 3: Train Linear Regression model
model = LinearRegression()
model.fit(X_train, y_train)
```

```python
# Step 4: Evaluate performance
y_pred = model.predict(X_test)
mae = mean_absolute_error(y_test, y_pred)
rmse = mean_squared_error(y_test, y_pred)
r2 = r2_score(y_test, y_pred)

print(f"Mean Absolute Error (MAE): {mae:.3f}")
print(f"Root Mean Squared Error (RMSE): {rmse:.3f}")
print(f"R² Score: {r2:.3f}")

# Step 5: Predict for a new example district
sample_values = [[5.0, 25, 6.0, 1.0, 1200, 3.0, 34.2, -118.3]]
sample_df = pd.DataFrame(sample_values, columns=X.columns)
pred_price = model.predict(sample_df)[0]
print(f"Predicted house value: ${pred_price * 100_000:,.0f}")
```

Example Output

```
Mean Absolute Error (MAE): 0.533
Root Mean Squared Error (RMSE): 0.556
R² Score: 0.576
Predicted house value: $244,415
```

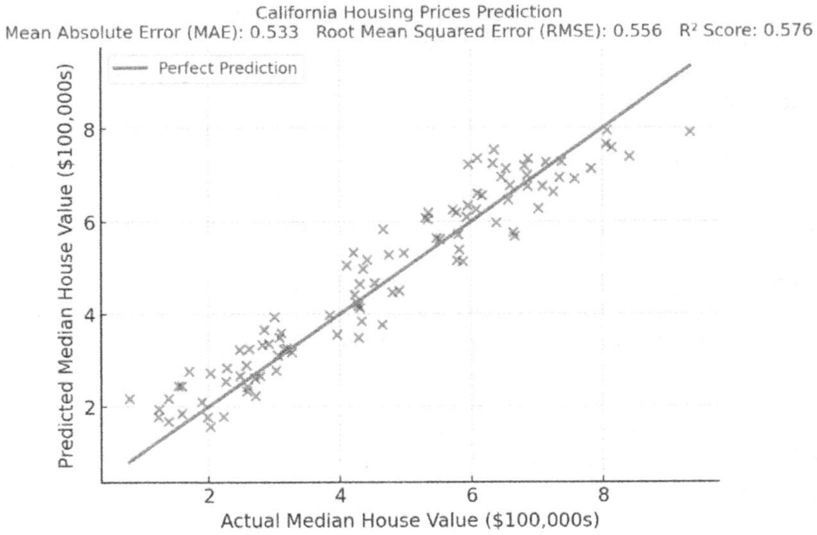

7.9 Summary

In this chapter, you explored **Supervised Learning**, one of the most widely used and practical areas of machine learning. You learned how supervised learning works by training models on labeled data and how it is used to make predictions on new, unseen inputs.

You examined the two main types of supervised learning problems: **regression**, where models predict continuous numeric values, and **classification**, where models predict discrete categories or labels. You also learned how these tasks are applied in real-world scenarios such as price prediction, spam detection, and customer analysis.

In addition, you explored how to **evaluate model performance**, compare different models, and save trained models for later use—an essential step in deploying machine learning systems beyond experimentation. Finally, through a hands-on project, you applied these concepts to build and test a supervised learning model using Python and scikit-learn.

With a solid understanding of supervised learning in place, you are now ready to move on to **unsupervised learning**, where models discover patterns in data without predefined labels.

Chapter 8:
Unsupervised Learning with Python

In the previous chapter, we explored *Supervised Learning,* where models learn from labeled data - meaning both the input features and the correct output values are known. But in many real-world situations, we don't have labeled data. We might have thousands of observations but no idea how to categorize or label them.

That's where **Unsupervised Learning** comes in.

8.1 What Is Unsupervised Learning?

Unsupervised learning is a type of machine learning that finds **patterns, relationships, or structures** in data **without predefined labels**. The model tries to understand the data's hidden structure by grouping or compressing it.

Algorithms are given raw, unlabeled data and tasked with finding similarities, differences, and patterns within it on their own.

Imagine you own an online store with thousands of customers, and you want to group them based on their purchasing habits. You don't know how many types of customers you have or what defines each type. An unsupervised algorithm can analyze the data and cluster customers with similar behavior — perhaps one group represents frequent buyers, another represents occasional shoppers, and so on.

Aspect	Supervised Learning	Unsupervised Learning
Input Data	Labeled (X, y)	Unlabeled (X only)
Goal	Predict outcomes	Discover patterns
Examples	Regression, Classification	Clustering, PCA
Evaluation	Accuracy, F1-score, MSE	Silhouette Score, Visualization

Types of Unsupervised Learning:

Unsupervised learning can be broadly divided into two main types:

- **Clustering** - Clustering organizes data points into **groups (clusters)**, such as grouping customers by purchasing patterns.

- **Dimensionality Reduction** - This technique reduces the number of features (variables) in a dataset while preserving as much information as possible. It's particularly useful when dealing with high-dimensional data, such as images or genetic data.

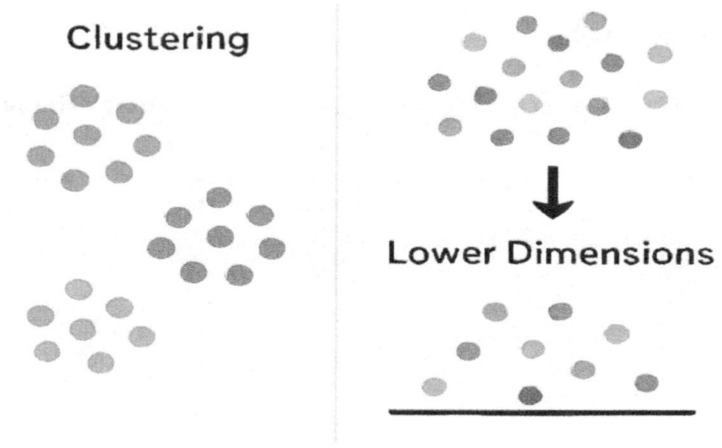

8.2 How Unsupervised Learning Works

In unsupervised learning, the model is trained on **unlabeled data** – meaning it must discover hidden structures or relationships on its own.
There are no predefined outputs or labels; the focus is on **finding patterns, grouping data**, or **reducing dimensions**.

Every unsupervised learning project typically follows these steps:

1. **Data Collection** – Gather relevant, unlabeled data such as customer activity logs, sensor readings, or images.
2. **Data Preparation** – Clean and preprocess the data by handling missing values, scaling numerical features, and removing noise.
3. **Training the Model** – Apply an unsupervised algorithm (like K-Means or PCA) to learn patterns or structure from the raw data.
4. **Grouping or Transformation** – The algorithm groups similar data points (clustering) or transforms features into a simpler form (dimensionality reduction).
5. **Evaluation and Interpretation** – Assess the model using metrics such as the Silhouette Score or visualize clusters to validate meaningful results.

This workflow helps reveal hidden insights, detect patterns, and simplify complex datasets – even when no labels or prior knowledge exist.

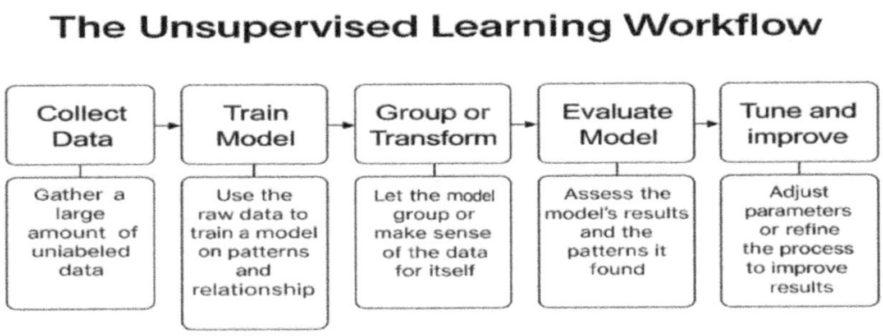

8.3 Clustering: Grouping Similar Data Points

Clustering is the most common form of unsupervised learning.

Its main goal is to **organize data into groups** (called *clusters*) where items within a cluster are similar to each other, and items from different clusters are dissimilar.

Think of clustering as letting your data organize itself into natural groups — no human labels required.

For example:

- In **marketing**, clustering can group customers by their buying behavior.
- In **healthcare**, it can group patients by symptoms or medical history.
- In **biology**, it can group genes by expression patterns.

The algorithm looks only at the features — not labels — and figures out which points belong together.

Popular Clustering Algorithms:

- **K-Means Clustering:** Divides data into fixed, spherical clusters
- **Hierarchical Clustering:** Builds a tree of nested clusters
- **DBSCAN (Density-Based Clustering):** Detects clusters of varying shape and density

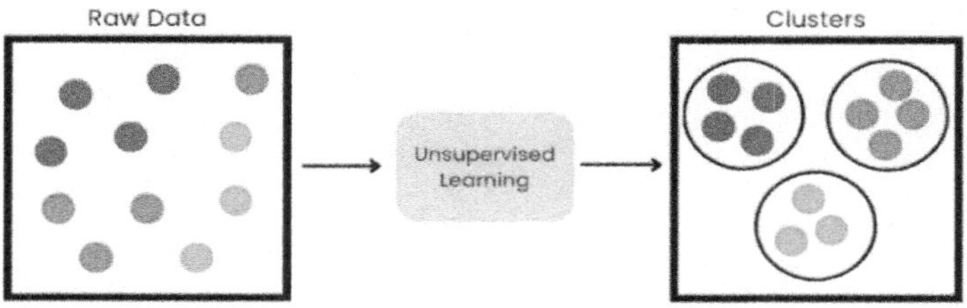

8.3.1 K-Means Clustering:

K-Means Clustering is an unsupervised machine learning algorithm and one of the simplest and most widely used clustering algorithms in machine learning. It aims to group similar data points into **K clusters**, where each cluster has a **centroid** (the mean of the data points in that group).

How K-Means Works:

1. **Initialize:** Choose the number of clusters (K) and randomly set initial centroids.
2. **Assign**: Group each data point with its nearest centroid using a distance metric (e.g., Euclidean distance).
3. **Update:** Recalculate centroids by finding the mean of all points in each group.
4. **Repeat:** Continue assigning and updating until centroids stabilize (convergence).

Python Example: K-Means Clustering

Below is a simple hands-on clustering example using **Iris dataset.**
The **Iris dataset**, which contains measurements of flower features such as sepal length, sepal width, petal length, and petal width, is a classic dataset for demonstrating clustering.
Even without the species labels, **K-Means** can group similar flowers together quite effectively.

Id	SepalLengthCm	SepalWidthCm	PetalLengthCm	PetalWidthCm
1	5.1	3.5	1.4	0.2
2	4.9	3.0	1.4	0.2
3	4.7	3.2	1.3	0.2
4	4.6	3.1	1.5	0.2
5	5.0	3.6	1.4	0.2
6	5.4	3.9	1.7	0.4
7	4.6	3.4	1.4	0.3
8	5.0	3.4	1.5	0.2
9	4.4	2.9	1.4	0.2
10	4.9	3.1	1.5	0.1

Here's Python example of K-Means clustering on the Iris dataset.

```
# Import Python libraries
from sklearn.cluster import KMeans
from sklearn.datasets import load_iris
import matplotlib.pyplot as plt
import pandas as pd

# Load the Iris dataset
iris = load_iris()
X = pd.DataFrame(iris.data, columns=iris.feature_names)

# Apply K-Means clustering
kmeans = KMeans(n_clusters=3, random_state=42)
y_kmeans = kmeans.fit_predict(X)

# Visualize the clusters
plt.scatter(
      X.iloc[:, 0], X.iloc[:, 1], c=y_kmeans,  cmap='viridis')
plt.xlabel('Sepal Length (cm)')
plt.ylabel('Sepal Width (cm)')
plt.title('K-Means Clustering on the Iris Dataset')
plt.show()
```

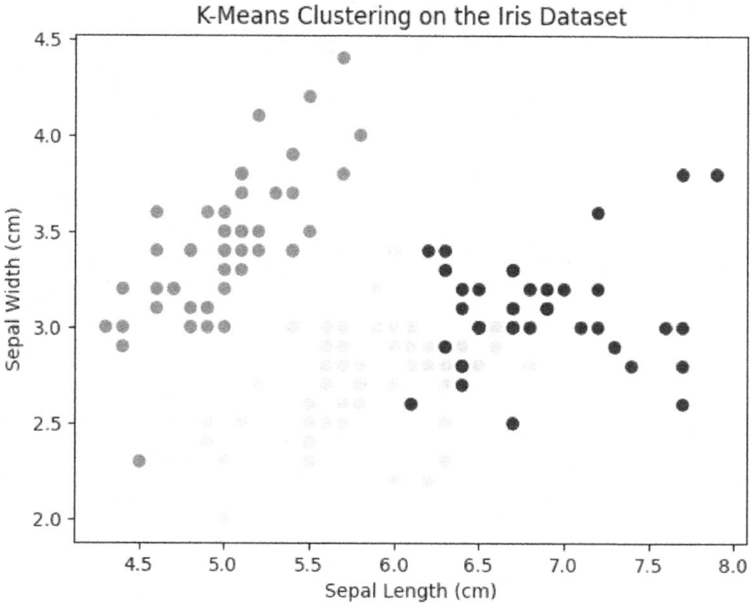

8.3.2 Hierarchical Clustering:

Hierarchical Clustering is an unsupervised method that groups data based on **similarity**. Unlike K-Means, it doesn't require a pre-set number of clusters; instead, it builds a **tree-like structure** called a **dendrogram** to show how data points merge at different levels. This is widely used in pattern recognition, customer segmentation, and gene analysis.

Example: Clustering Fruits by Weight Imagine grouping four fruits: Apple (100g), Banana (120g), Cherry (50g), and Grape (30g).

1. **Individual Clusters:** Start with each fruit as its own group.
2. **Initial Merge:** The most similar weights—Grape and Cherry—form the first cluster.
3. **Second Merge:** The next closest pair—Apple and Banana—are grouped together.
4. **Final Hierarchy:** The two groups merge into a single dendrogram containing all four fruits.

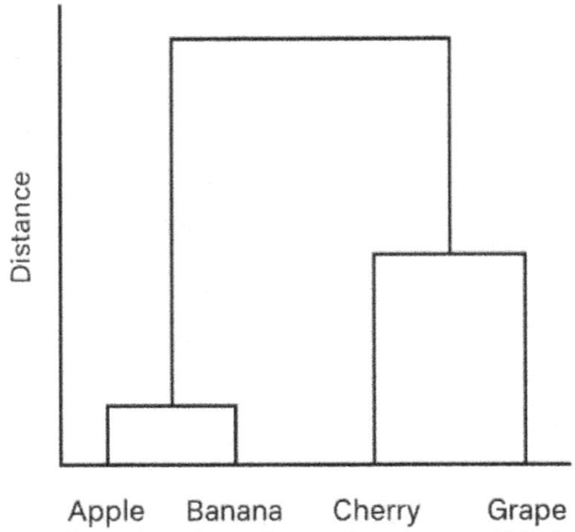

8.4 Dimensionality Reduction: Simplifying Complex Data

In real-world AI problems, datasets often contain a large number of features. While more features may seem useful, they can introduce noise, increase computational cost, and make it harder for models to learn meaningful patterns. **Dimensionality reduction** addresses this challenge by reducing the number of input features while preserving the most important information in the data.

One of the main reasons for applying dimensionality reduction is **improved efficiency**. Models trained on high-dimensional data often require more memory and processing time. Reducing dimensionality can speed up training and make models easier to interpret. It can also help reduce overfitting by removing redundant or irrelevant features.

Dimensionality reduction is commonly used for **data visualization**, where high-dimensional data is projected into two or three dimensions to reveal patterns, clusters, and outliers.

Several techniques are commonly used for dimensionality reduction. Among the most popular are **Principal Component Analysis (PCA)** and **Singular Value Decomposition (SVD)**. These methods transform the original features into a smaller set of new features that capture the most significant variations in the data.

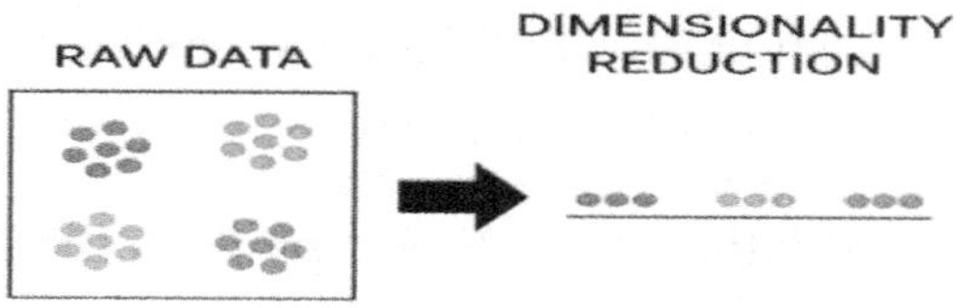

For example:

- In **finance**, dimensionality reduction can compress thousands of market indicators into a few key economic factors.
- In **healthcare**, it can reduce complex genetic data into principal components that highlight major disease patterns.
- In **image processing**, it can simplify high-resolution images while preserving essential visual features.
- In **cybersecurity**, it can reduce network traffic features to detect anomalies more efficiently.

Dimensionality reduction is often applied before clustering or visualization and may also serve as a preprocessing step for other machine learning models. A deeper treatment of these techniques will be covered later in the book.

8.5 Evaluation of Unsupervised Models

After performing clustering or dimensionality reduction, it's important to check **how good the model's results are** — even though there are no labels to compare against.

Here are some metrics used to measure clustering performance:

- **Silhouette Score:** Measures how similar each point is to its own cluster compared to other clusters. The score ranges from -1 to +1. Higher values indicate better-defined clusters.

- **Davies–Bouldin Index**: Measures the average similarity ratio between each cluster and its most similar neighbor. Lower values indicate better clustering.

- **Visual Validation**: Sometimes, plotting the clusters gives a more intuitive sense of quality than metrics alone.

8.6 Hands-On Project: Customer Segmentation using Unsupervised Learning

In this project, we'll apply **unsupervised learning** to a real-world scenario — **customer segmentation**. Businesses often use segmentation to group customers based on their behavior, spending patterns, or preferences.

Project Goal

To group customers into meaningful clusters using their **annual income** and **spending score** and visualize the results.

Steps

1. **Create a small sample dataset** using pandas to represent customer information.
2. **Select key features** — *Annual Income* and *Spending Score* — for clustering.
3. **Scale the features** so both variables are on a similar range.
4. **Apply K-Means Clustering** to group customers into distinct segments.
5. **Visualize the clusters** using a scatter plot to observe customer groupings.
6. **Evaluate clustering quality** using the **Silhouette Score**.

Python Code: Customer Segmentation

```
import pandas as pd
import matplotlib.pyplot as plt
from sklearn.cluster import KMeans
from sklearn.preprocessing import StandardScaler
from sklearn.metrics import silhouette_score

# Step 1: Create a small sample dataset
data = {
'CustomerID': [1, 2, 3, 4, 5, 6, 7, 8],
'Gender':['Male','Female','Female','Male','Female',
          'Male','Female','Male'],
'Age': [19,21,20,23,31,35,40,26],
'Annual Income (k$)': [15,15,16,17,18,25,40,60],
'Spending Score (1-100)': [39,81,76,77,40,65,80,50]
}

df = pd.DataFrame(data)

# Step 2: Select features for clustering
X = df[['Annual Income (k$)', 'Spending Score (1-100)']]

# Step 3: Scale the features so contribute equally
scaler = StandardScaler()
X_scaled = scaler.fit_transform(X)

# Step 4: Apply K-Means Clustering
kmeans = KMeans(n_clusters=3, random_state=42)
labels = kmeans.fit_predict(X_scaled)
df['Cluster'] = labels

# Step 5: Visualize the clusters
plt.figure(figsize=(8, 6))
plt.scatter(X_scaled[:, 0], X_scaled[:, 1], c=labels,
            cmap='viridis', s=80)
plt.title('Customer Segmentation using K-Means')
plt.xlabel('Annual Income (Standardized)')
plt.ylabel('Spending Score (Standardized)')
plt.show()

# Step 6: Evaluate clustering quality
score = silhouette_score(X_scaled, labels)
print(f"\nSilhouette Score: {score:.2f}")

# Step 7: Display final dataset with cluster labels
print("\nFinal Dataset with Cluster Labels:")
print(df)
```

Expected Output:

- A colorful **scatter plot** with 3 distinct customer groups.
- A **Silhouette Score** (usually between 0.5–0.7) indicating cluster separation.
- A final DataFrame showing each customer's **cluster assignment**.

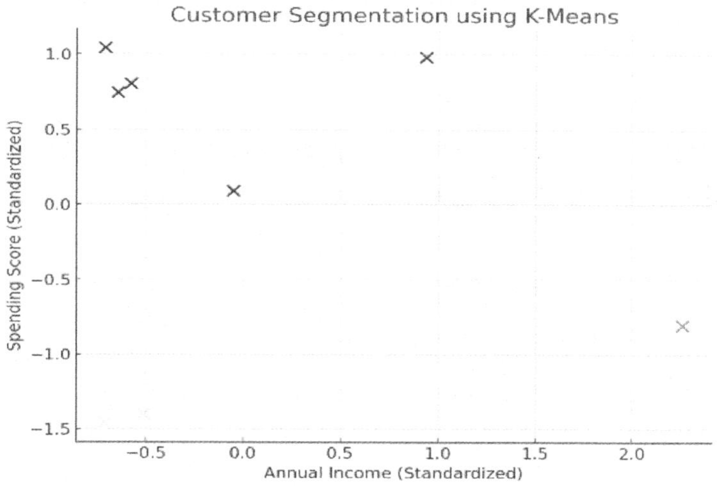

Final Dataset with Cluster Labels:

CustomerID	Gender	Age	Annual Income (k$)	Spending Score (1-100)	Cluster
1	Male	19	15	39	2
2	Female	21	15	81	0
3	Female	20	16	76	0
4	Male	23	17	77	0
5	Female	31	18	40	2
6	Male	35	25	65	0
7	Female	40	40	80	0
8	Male	26	60	50	1

8.7 Summary

In this chapter, you explored **unsupervised learning**, a machine learning approach that discovers patterns in data without using labeled outputs. You learned how unsupervised methods help reveal hidden structure in datasets and how they differ from supervised learning techniques.

You examined two key unsupervised learning techniques: **clustering**, which groups similar data points, and **dimensionality reduction**, which simplifies complex datasets by reducing the number of features. You also learned why evaluating unsupervised models can be challenging and how basic evaluation ideas are applied in practice.

Through a hands-on project, you applied these concepts **to customer segmentation**, gaining practical experience in grouping data and interpreting the resulting patterns. With an understanding of how models learn structure from unlabeled data, you are now ready to move on to **deep learning and neural networks**, where models learn increasingly complex representations of data.

Part III – Deep Learning & Neural Networks

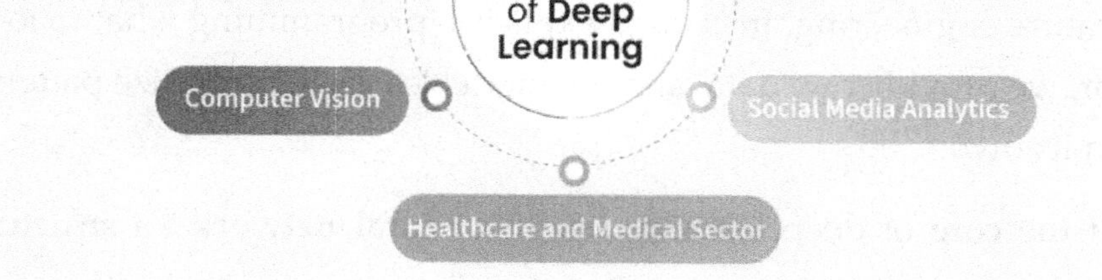

Chapter 9: Introduction to Neural Networks & Deep Learning

In the previous chapters, you learned how machines can be trained using algorithms like regression, decision trees, clustering, and dimensionality reduction. These traditional **machine learning** methods are powerful, but they have limitations—especially when dealing with **high-dimensional data** such as images, video, and natural language.

To overcome these challenges, researchers developed **Deep Learning**, a specialized branch of machine learning inspired by how the **human brain** processes information. Deep learning models can automatically learn features from data, reducing the need for manual feature engineering. Instead of explicitly programming what to look for, we provide raw data, and the model learns to recognize patterns on its own.

At the core of deep learning lies the **neural network**—a structure made up of interconnected "neurons" that pass information and learn through repetition. Neural networks are the foundation of many modern AI breakthroughs, from **voice assistants like Alexa and Siri** to **image recognition, self-driving cars, and ChatGPT-style language models**.

In this chapter, you'll explore how neural networks work, understand how they learn, and build your very first deep learning model using **TensorFlow and Keras**. This marks the beginning of our journey into the world of **Deep Learning**, where AI starts to see, hear, and understand the world in ways that mimic human intelligence.

9.1 What Are Neural Networks & Deep Learning

A **neural network** is a computational model inspired by how the **human brain** works. Just as our brains contain billions of neurons that transmit signals, a neural network consists of **artificial neurons** (or "nodes") connected together in layers. Each neuron receives input, processes it, and passes output to the next neuron — gradually transforming the data as it flows through the network.

At its core, a neural network tries to **learn patterns** in data. For example:

- If you feed it pictures of cats and dogs, it will learn to tell them apart.
- If you show it thousands of handwritten digits, it can learn to recognize any new one it hasn't seen before.
- If you train it on text data, it can predict words or generate new sentences.

This ability to learn **representations automatically**—without being explicitly programmed—is what makes neural networks so powerful.

How It Works (In Simple Terms)

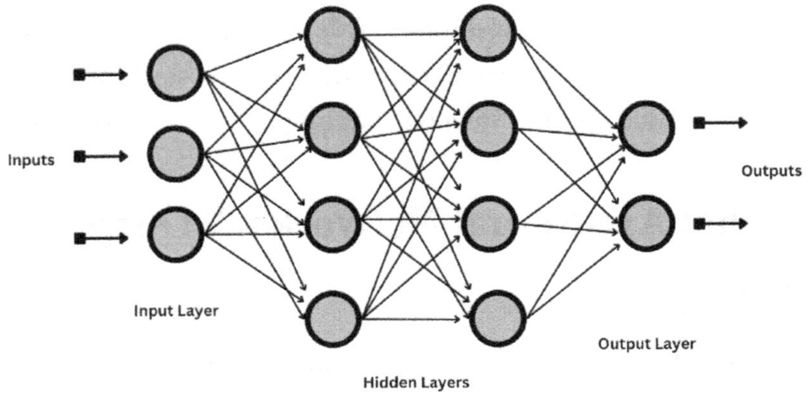

Think of a neural network as a series of decision makers:

1. **Input Layer** – receives raw data (like pixel values, text tokens, or numbers).
2. **Hidden Layers** – perform mathematical transformations and extract meaningful features.
3. **Output Layer** – produces the final result (like a category label or a numeric prediction).

Each connection between neurons has an associated **weight**, which represents how important that connection is. During training, the network adjusts these weights to improve its predictions — a process similar to how we learn from experience.

What Makes It "Deep"?

When a neural network has **many hidden layers**, it's called a **deep neural network** — hence the term **"Deep Learning."**

Simple Neural Network:

Input Layer → Hidden Layer → Output Layer

Deep Neural Network:

Input Layer → Hidden Layer 1 → Hidden Layer 2 → ... → Hidden Layer N → Output Layer

Deep learning is not a new concept, but recent advances in **computing power (GPUs)**, **large datasets**, and **optimization algorithms** have made it practical and extremely successful.

Why Deep Learning Matters

Deep learning has revolutionized modern AI by achieving human-level (and sometimes superhuman) performance in many tasks:

- **Image Recognition:** Identifying objects, faces, and scenes.
- **Speech Recognition:** Converting voice to text in real time.
- **Natural Language Processing (NLP):** Powering chatbots and translation systems.
- **Autonomous Systems:** Helping self-driving cars understand their surroundings.

In short, deep learning enables machines to **perceive, understand, and act** — making it the driving force behind today's AI revolution.

9.2 How Neural Networks Learn

Once you understand a single neuron, the next step is to see how many of them work together in layers to form a neural network. This is where deep learning gets its power — from stacking multiple layers of neurons that learn patterns from data automatically.

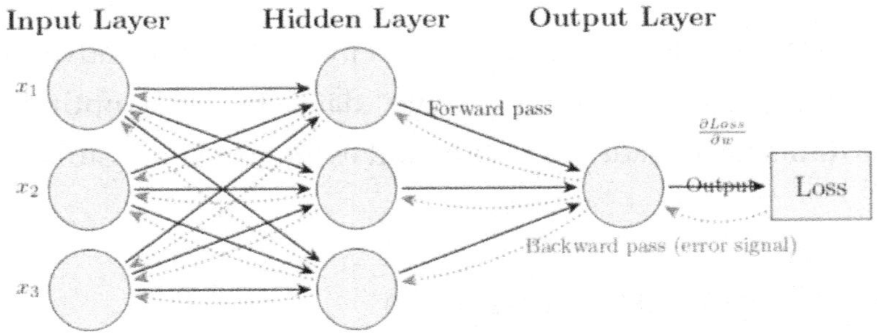

1. Layers in a Neural Network:

A neural network is made up of several layers, each with its own role:

- **Input Layer:**
  This is where data enters the network. For example, if you're training the network on images, each pixel becomes an input value.
- **Hidden Layers:**
  These layers transform and process the input data. The first layer might detect simple features (like edges or colors), while deeper layers combine those features to recognize shapes, objects, or even faces.
- **Output Layer:**
  The final layer gives the result — such as predicting whether an image shows a cat or a dog.

Each connection between neurons has a **weight**, which represents how strongly one neuron influences another. During training, these weights are adjusted so the network becomes better at making predictions.

2. Activation Functions: Bringing the Network to Life:

In real-world data, relationships are rarely simple or linear. **Activation functions** help the network handle these complexities.

They decide whether a neuron should "activate" or not based on the input it receives. Without them, the network would behave like a simple calculator, unable to learn complex patterns.

You can think of an activation function like a **decision-maker** inside each neuron. If the input is meaningful enough, the neuron "fires" (sends the signal forward). If not, it stays quiet.

What matters most is that activation functions allow neural networks to understand patterns that are too complex for traditional algorithms.

3. Backpropagation: Learning from Mistakes:

Training a neural network means teaching it to make better predictions over time. **Backpropagation** is the algorithm that enables neural networks to learn that involves two main steps:

- **Forward Pass:**
  The data moves through the network from the input to the output layer. The network makes a prediction based on its current knowledge.
- **Backward Pass (Learning from Mistakes):**
  The prediction is compared to the correct answer. If the prediction is wrong, the network slightly adjusts its internal connections (weights) to reduce future errors.

This process happens over and over — sometimes thousands of times — until the network gets really good at its task.

You can think of it like a student taking multiple practice tests. After each test, they review their mistakes, learn from them, and improve their score next time. The more they practice, the better they perform.

4. The Learning Cycle

The network continues this process for many **training rounds**, also called **epochs**. Each round improves its understanding of the data. In the beginning, the network might make a lot of mistakes, but over time, its predictions become more accurate.

9.3 When to Use Deep Learning

Now that you understand how neural networks work, an important question arises: **When should you use deep learning, and when is traditional machine learning enough?**

Not every problem requires a deep learning model. In fact, for many tasks, simpler algorithms like **linear regression**, **decision trees**, or **random forests** perform just as well — and are faster to train and easier to interpret. However, there are specific situations where deep learning truly shines.

1. **When You Have a Large Amount of Data:**

Deep learning models need lots of data to perform well. They learn patterns automatically — but only if they have enough examples to learn from.
For example:

- If you have millions of labeled images, a deep neural network can recognize objects better than traditional models.
- If you only have a few hundred samples, simpler models like logistic regression or support vector machines may give better results.

Rule of thumb: The more data you have, the more useful deep learning becomes.

2. **When the Problem Is Complex or Unstructured:**

Deep learning is particularly powerful for **unstructured data** — data that doesn't fit neatly into rows and columns.

Examples include:

- **Images** (for object detection, facial recognition)
- **Text** (for sentiment analysis, translation, chatbots)
- **Audio** (for speech recognition, music generation)
- **Video** (for motion tracking, autonomous driving)

Traditional machine learning struggles with such data because it requires manual feature extraction — deciding what aspects of the data are important. Deep learning models, on the other hand, **learn those features automatically**.

3. **When Accuracy Is More Important Than Speed:**

Deep learning models often achieve higher accuracy but take more time and resources to train. If your goal is the *best possible accuracy* and you can afford the computational cost, deep learning is usually the better choice. However, for smaller or time-sensitive projects, a simpler model might be more practical.

4. **When You Have Access to Powerful Hardware:**

Deep learning involves intensive computations that benefit from specialized hardware like **GPUs (Graphics Processing Units)** or **TPUs (Tensor Processing Units)**. If you have access to these, training deep models becomes much faster and more efficient. Without them, training may take hours or even days on a regular computer.

5. **When You Need Feature Learning:**

In traditional machine learning, you often have to design input features manually — deciding which variables matter. Deep learning models can discover these features on their own, especially in image and language tasks. This makes them excellent for problems where it's hard to define features upfront.

Key Differences: Traditional ML vs. Deep Learning

Aspect	Traditional ML	Deep Learning
Feature Engineering	Manual	Automatic
Data Requirements	Works with smaller datasets	Requires large datasets
Computational Power	Less intensive	GPU-intensive
Interpretability	More interpretable	"Black box" (harder to interpret)
Performance	Limited	Excellent (images, speech, text)
Training Time	Faster	Slower

In Summary:

Use **deep learning** when:

- You have a **large, complex dataset** (especially images, text, or audio).
- You care most about **accuracy and performance**.
- You have access to **powerful hardware** (like GPUs).
- The problem requires **automatic feature extraction**.

Stick with **traditional machine learning** when:

- You have **limited data** or **fewer computing resources**.
- You need **interpretability** and **faster training**.
- The task is relatively **simple** and structured (like predicting sales or classifying tabular data).

9.4 Introduction to TensorFlow and Keras

Building and training a neural network from scratch using only Python and NumPy is a great learning experience — but it can quickly become complex for real-world problems. This is where **deep learning frameworks** like **TensorFlow** and **Keras** come in. They simplify the entire process, allowing you to focus on designing and training models rather than worrying about the low-level math behind them.

What Is TensorFlow?

TensorFlow is an open-source deep learning framework developed by **Google**. It's designed for building and deploying large-scale machine learning and deep learning models.
TensorFlow allows you to:

- Define and train neural networks easily.
- Run models on CPUs, GPUs, or TPUs for high performance.
- Deploy trained models to production environments (mobile apps, web services, etc.)

The name *TensorFlow* comes from the way data moves through the system:
"tensors" (multidimensional data arrays) *flow* between operations in a computational graph.

What Is Keras?

Keras is a **high-level API** built on top of TensorFlow. The beauty of Keras is its simplicity. You can build complex neural networks with just a few lines of code, making it perfect for both beginners and experienced practitioners who want to prototype quickly.

Keras provides:

- Simple and readable syntax
- Ready-to-use layers (Dense, Convolutional, Recurrent, etc.)
- Built-in tools for training, evaluating, and saving models

In fact, Keras is now **officially integrated into TensorFlow**, so you'll often import it as:

```
from tensorflow import keras
```

How TensorFlow and Keras Work Together

When you build a model using Keras, it communicates with TensorFlow behind the scenes. TensorFlow handles the heavy lifting — mathematical operations, optimization, and hardware acceleration — while Keras provides a clean and easy way to define and manage models.

Install TensorFlow (which includes Keras), use pip:

```
pip install tensorflow
```

Why Use TensorFlow and Keras?

Here's why they're ideal for beginners and professionals alike:

- **Ease of use:** Build models quickly without deep math knowledge.
- **Flexibility:** Supports simple prototypes and large-scale production systems.
- **Performance:** Utilizes GPUs for fast computation.
- **Community support:** Huge ecosystem of tutorials, datasets, and pre-trained models.

9.5 Hands-On: Building Your First Neural Network with Keras

In this project, you'll create a simple deep learning model using **TensorFlow and Keras** to recognize handwritten digits (0–9) from the **MNIST dataset.**

The goal is to show how easily you can build and train a model — even without complex math or theory.

Project Goal:

Train a neural network to correctly identify handwritten digits with high accuracy. MNIST dataset contains 70,000 images of handwritten digits (0-9), each 28x28 pixels. We'll explore the theory and details of the following example in Chapter-10.

Python Code: Your First Neural Network with Keras

```
# Step 1: Import the required libraries and mnist dataset

import tensorflow as tf
from tensorflow import keras
from tensorflow.keras import layers
from tensorflow.keras.datasets import mnist

# Step 2: Load the MNIST dataset

(x_train, y_train), (x_test, y_test) = mnist.load_data()

# Step 3: Normalize the data. Scale pixel values (0-255)
# to  between 0 and 1 for faster training

x_train = x_train / 255.0
x_test = x_test / 255.0
```

```
# Step 4: Build the neural network model
# We'll use a simple Sequential model with three layers
# Input layer converts each 28x28 image into a 1D array
# Hidden layer with 128 neurons
# Output layer for 10 classes (digits 0-9)

model = keras.Sequential([
    layers.Flatten(input_shape=(28, 28)),
    layers.Dense(128, activation='relu'),
    layers.Dense(10, activation='softmax')
])

# Step 5: Compile the model
# Define how the model learns: optimizer, loss function,
# and metric

model.compile(
    optimizer='adam',
    loss='sparse_categorical_crossentropy',
    metrics=['accuracy']
)

# Step 6: Train the model
# Fit the model on training data for 5 passes (epochs)

model.fit(x_train, y_train, epochs=5)

# Step 7: Evaluate the model
# Check how well it performs on unseen test data

test_loss, test_acc = model.evaluate(x_test, y_test)
print("Test accuracy:", test_acc)

# Step 8: Make predictions (optional)
# Predict the digit for the first test image

predictions = model.predict(x_test)
print("Predicted digit:", tf.argmax(predictions[0]).numpy())
```

Expected Output:

After training for a few minutes, you should see results similar to this:

```
Epoch 1/5
1875/1875 ━━━━━ 8s 4ms/step - accuracy: 0.8787 - loss: 0.4318
Epoch 2/5
1875/1875 ━━━━━ 5s 3ms/step - accuracy: 0.9636 - loss: 0.1221
Epoch 3/5
1875/1875 ━━━━━ 6s 3ms/step - accuracy: 0.9757 - loss: 0.0794
Epoch 4/5
1875/1875 ━━━━━ 5s 3ms/step - accuracy: 0.9822 - loss: 0.0597
Epoch 5/5
1875/1875 ━━━━━ 5s 3ms/step - accuracy: 0.9880 - loss: 0.0417
```

Test accuracy: 0.9753000140190125
Predicted digit: 7

That means your model correctly classifies around **97–98%** of the handwritten digits — pretty amazing for such a simple network!

Key Takeaways:

- You just built your **first working neural network** using Keras.
- The model learned from examples without you explicitly telling it what a "7" or "8" looks like.
- Deep learning models like this form the foundation for advanced applications such as image recognition, speech processing, and even ChatGPT-like systems.

9.6 Summary

In this chapter, we've explored the fascinating world of neural networks and deep learning:

- ✓ Introduced the fundamentals of deep learning and how neural networks mimic the human brain.
- ✓ Learned how neural networks process data through layers of interconnected neurons.
- ✓ Explored activation functions, forward/backward propagation, and how networks learn by adjusting weights.
- ✓ Understood when to use deep learning (large, complex, unstructured data) and when simpler ML models are more suitable.
- ✓ Built and trained your first neural network using TensorFlow and Keras to recognize handwritten digits.

Chapter 10:
Building and Training Deep Learning Models

10.1 Understanding Deep Learning Architectures

Deep learning becomes powerful not just because it uses neural networks — but because it uses **deep architectures**. These architectures define how layers are arranged, how data flows, and what kind of patterns the network can learn.

At a high level, a deep learning architecture describes:

- How many layers the network has
- What types of layers are used
- How these layers are connected
- How information moves from input to output

The simplest deep learning model is the **feedforward neural network** (also called an Artificial Neural Network or ANN). This was the type you built in Chapter 9. In this architecture, data flows in one direction:

Input Layer → Hidden Layers → Output Layer

Feedforward networks are great for basic tasks like classification or regression, but real-world problems often require more specialized architectures.

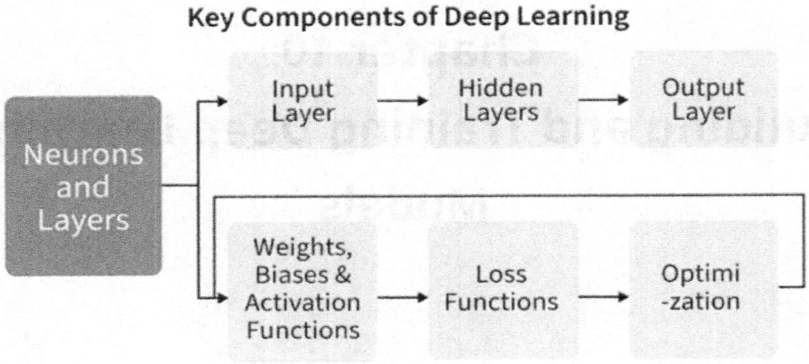

Common Deep Learning Architectures:

1. **Convolutional Neural Networks (CNNs)**
   Designed for image-related tasks. CNNs learn patterns such as edges, textures, and shapes by sliding small filters across the image. They are widely used in facial recognition, medical imaging, and self-driving cars.
2. **Recurrent Neural Networks (RNNs)**
   Ideal for sequence data where order matters—such as text, speech, and time series. RNNs have a "memory" mechanism that allows them to carry information from previous steps. Advanced variants like **LSTMs** improve learning long-term patterns.
3. **Transformers**
   The most modern and powerful architecture, used in large language models (LLM) like GPT and BERT. Transformers rely on an "attention" mechanism to focus on important parts of the input, making them extremely effective for text, translation, and even multimodal tasks like vision + language.

Each architecture solves different types of problems:

Task Type	Best Architecture
Images & video	CNNs
Text & sequences	RNNs / LSTMs
Modern NLP (Natural Language Processing)	Transformers
Simple numeric data	Feedforward ANN

Selecting the right architecture is crucial for high performance. As you progress, you will learn to build, train, and optimize these models for real-world AI tasks.

10.2 Training Concepts: Layers, Epochs, Batches and Hyperparameters

To train a model, you need to understand a few core components. These determine *how* the model learns and *how well* it performs.

1. Layers: The Building Blocks of Neural Networks

A neural network is made up of multiple types of layers, each responsible for transforming data into more meaningful representations.

- **Input Layer:** Receives the raw data (e.g., the 28x28 pixels of an image).
- **Hidden Layers:** The main computational layers that learn patterns. A **deep** network has many of these.
  - **Dense Layer:** Connects every neuron to every neuron in the next layer.
  - **Dropout Layer:** Prevents overfitting by randomly disabling neurons during training.
- **Output Layer:** Gives the final prediction (e.g., which clothing item is in the image).

2. Hyperparameters: Controlling the Learning

Hyperparameters are settings you choose to control the learning process. Choosing good hyperparameters can dramatically improve model accuracy.

Hyperparameter	What It Controls and Impact
Learning Rate	How big the weight updates are during training. **Impact:** Too high → unstable, erratic learning. Too low → training is very slow.
Batch Size	How many data samples the model processes at once. (e.g., 32 images). **Impact:** Affects memory usage and learning stability.
Number of Epochs	How many times the model sees the entire training dataset. **Impact:** Too many → Overfitting (memorization).

3. Epochs and Batches: The Training Flow

To make training efficient, data is processed in chunks.

- **Batch:** A small subset of the training data (e.g., 32 or 64 samples) processed simultaneously. The model updates its weights after each batch.
- **Epoch:** One complete pass through the entire training dataset.

If you train for 10 epochs, the model has seen every piece of training data 10 times.

10.3 Loss Functions and Optimizers

To train a deep learning model effectively, two components play a central role: **the loss function** and **the optimizer**. Together, they determine **how well the model learns** and **how quickly it improves** during training.

Loss Functions: Measuring Model Error

A loss function tells the neural network *how far off* its predictions are from the correct answers. During training, the goal is simple:

Lower the loss → Better the model.

After each training step, the model calculates the loss and uses it to adjust internal weights.

Different tasks require different loss functions:

Task Type	Loss Function	Purpose
Classification	Crossentropy (Binary or Categorical)	Measures the difference between the predicted probability distribution and the true distribution.
Regression	Mean Squared Error (MSE)	Measures the average squared difference between predictions and actual values. Penalizes larger errors more heavily.

Optimizers: How the Model Learns

The **Optimizer** is the algorithm that decides how to change the network's internal **weights** to reduce the loss. It is the "engine" of the learning process.

- **How it Works:** The optimizer uses a technique called **backpropagation** to calculate which weights contributed most to the error (loss) and updates them in the direction that lowers the loss.
- **Adam (Adaptive Moment Estimation)**: is the most popular and recommended optimizer for most modern deep learning problems because it automatically adjusts the learning rate for each weight, leading to faster, more stable convergence.

How Loss Functions and Optimizers Work Together:

Training loop overview:

1. Model makes a prediction
2. Loss function calculates the error
3. Optimizer updates weights to reduce that error
4. Repeat for every batch, across multiple epochs

This cycle continues until the loss is low enough and the model performs well.

Keras Example: Compiling the Model

The compile step brings the loss and optimizer together:

```
model.compile(
    optimizer='adam', # The learning strategy
    loss='sparse_categorical_crossentropy', # What to minimize
    metrics=['accuracy'] # What to track
)
```

Here is the Summary of Deep Learning Concepts from Section 10.2 and 10.3:

Concept	What It Controls / Describes
Layers	Define the architecture and structure of the neural network.
Batches	Determine how much data the model processes at one time.
Epochs	Control how many times the model sees the entire dataset during training.
Hyperparameters	Control the learning process and overall model behavior.
Loss Functions	Measure how far off the model's predictions are from the true values.
Optimizers	Adjust the model's weights to reduce the loss.
Learning Rate	Determines how fast or slow the model learns during training.

Understanding these components will help you train stable, accurate models and troubleshoot issues in future chapters and hands-project.

10.4 Activation Functions

In neural networks, the activation function decides how a neuron responds to input and is used to improve performance of the model. The activation function is a mathematical expression that decides whether the input should pass through a neuron or not based on its significance. It also provides non-linearity to networks. Without activation function, the neural network becomes a simple linear regression model.

There are several types of activation functions:

Activation Function	Use Case
ReLU **(Rectified Linear Unit)**	Most Common. Used in Hidden Layers. It's fast, simple, and effective. Output is 0 for negative input, and non-zero for positive input.
Sigmoid	Binary Classification Output. Compresses any input value into a range between 0 and 1. Useful for the output layer when predicting a probability.
Softmax	Multi-Class Classification Output. Converts the final layer's outputs into a set of probabilities that sum up to 1. Used when classifying 3 or more classes (e.g., the 10 fashion items).

10.5 Evaluating Model Performance

Training a model is only the first step. The real question is: **How well does it work on new, unseen data?**

To answer that, we use a few simple evaluation tools.

1. Training, Validation, and Test Data:

When building a model, we split the data into three parts:

- **Training data** – the model learns from this.
- **Validation data** – used during training to check if the model is improving or overfitting.
- **Test data** – used at the very end to measure real, unbiased performance.

Splitting the data prevents the model from simply memorizing the training data.

2. Common Evaluation Metrics:

Different tasks need different ways to measure performance.

For classification (predicting categories):

- **Accuracy** – How many predictions were correct?
- **Precision & Recall** – Useful when some classes are rare or more important.
- **F1-score** – A balanced score that combines precision and recall.
- **Confusion Matrix** – A simple table showing correct and incorrect predictions for each class.

For regression (predicting numbers):

- **MAE (Mean Absolute Error)** – Average absolute difference between prediction and actual value.
- **MSE (Mean Squared Error)** – Like MAE, but penalizes large errors more.
- **R^2 Score** – Measures how well the model explains the variation in the data.

3. Tracking Progress with Loss Curves:

During training, we usually look at two curves:

- **Training loss** – how well the model is learning from training data
- **Validation loss** – how well it performs on unseen data

These curves help us spot problems:

- **Underfitting** → both losses are high
- **Overfitting** → training loss drops, but validation loss increases
- **Good training** → both curves decrease and stay close

This helps us decide when to stop training and whether the model is too simple or too complex.

4. Evaluating the Model in Keras:

Keras makes evaluation very easy:

```
test_loss, test_acc = model.evaluate(x_test, y_test)
print("Test accuracy:", test_acc)
```

The evaluate() function returns the loss and any metrics you chose when compiling the model.

5. How Do You Know the Model Is "Good Enough"?

A model is usually ready when:

- Training and validation results are similar
- Overfitting is under control
- Test accuracy (or error) meets your goals
- Predictions look reasonable in real situations

The goal is not perfection, but **good, reliable performance**.

10.6 Hands-On: Building a Deep Neural Network with Keras

In this project, you will build a deeper and more powerful neural network than the one introduced in Chapter 9. You will train the model on the Fashion MNIST dataset — a more challenging dataset than handwritten digits.

The goal is to show you how all the concepts from this chapter come together to create a robust, high-performing deep learning model.

Project Goal:

In this project, you will build a **deep neural network** to classify clothing items from the **Fashion MNIST** dataset.

- Each image is **28×28 pixels**, grayscale.
- There are **10 classes** (T-shirt, trouser, dress, etc.).
- We'll build a small but powerful model using **Dense layers** and **ReLU / Softmax** activations.

Class	Label
0	T-shirt/top
1	Trouser
2	Pullover
3	Dress
4	Coat
5	Sandal
6	Shirt
7	Sneaker
8	Bag
9	Ankle boot

Python Code:

```
# Step 1: Import the libraries
import tensorflow as tf
from tensorflow import keras
from tensorflow.keras import layers
from tensorflow.keras.datasets import fashion_mnist

# Step 2: Load the Fashion MNIST dataset
(x_train, y_train), (x_test, y_test) =  fashion_mnist.load_data()

# Step 3: Scale pixel values (0-255) to between 0 and 1
x_train = x_train / 255.0
x_test = x_test / 255.0

# Step 4: Build a Deeper neural network model
model = keras.Sequential([
   layers.Flatten(input_shape=(28, 28)),# Input layer
   layers.Dense(128, activation='relu'),# Hidden layer 1
   layers.Dense(64, activation='relu'), # Hidden layer 2
   layers.Dense(10, activation='softmax') # Output layer
])

# Step 5: Compile the model
model.compile(
   optimizer='adam',
   loss='sparse_categorical_crossentropy',
   metrics=['accuracy']
)

# Step 6: Train the model
history = model.fit(
   x_train, y_train,
   epochs=10,
   batch_size=64,
   validation_split=0.2

# Step 7: Evaluate the model
test_loss, test_acc = model.evaluate(x_test, y_test)
print("Test accuracy:", test_acc)

# Step 8: Make a prediction with the trained model
predictions = model.predict(x_test)
```

```
# Convert prediction probabilities into a class label
predicted_class = tf.argmax(predictions[0]).numpy()

print("Predicted class for first test image:", predicted_class)
print("Actual class:", y_test[0])
```

Expected Output

When you train the model, you should see something similar to the following (your numbers may vary slightly):

```
Epoch 1/10
750/750 ━━━━━━━━━━ 6s  accuracy: 0.78  val_accuracy: 0.84
Epoch 2/10
750/750 ━━━━━━━━━━ 5s  accuracy: 0.86  val_accuracy: 0.87
Epoch 3/10
750/750 ━━━━━━━━━━ 5s  accuracy: 0.88  val_accuracy: 0.88
...
Epoch 10/10
750/750 ━━━━━━━━━━ 5s  accuracy: 0.90  val_accuracy: 0.89
```

Final test accuracy is usually around:

```
313/313 ━━━━ 1s
Test accuracy: 0.88
```

And when you make a prediction:

```
1/1 ━━━━━━ 0s
Predicted class for first test image: 9
Actual class: 9
```

Example Output:

These results show that the model is performing well, with around **88–90% accuracy** on unseen test images.

What this example shows:

- How to load and scale image data
- How to build a deep neural network with Keras
- How to compile, train, and evaluate a model
- How concepts like layers, epochs, batches, optimizer, loss, and activation functions work together in practice

10.7 Saving, Loading & Reusing Models

After training a deep learning model, one of the most important steps is saving it for future use. You may want to:

- Reuse the model without retraining
- Deploy it in a real application
- Continue training later
- Share it with others
- Move it to another machine

Keras makes all of this incredibly simple. In this section, you'll learn how to properly save, load, and reuse your trained models.

1. Saving Your Model in Keras:

Keras provides two main ways to save a model:

A. Save the Entire Model (Recommended)

This saves Architecture, Weights, Optimizer state and Training configuration

```
model.save("fashion_model.h5")
```

B. Save Only the Weights

```
model.save_weights("fashion_weights.h5")
```

Useful if you want to recreate architecture manually

2. Loading a Saved Model:

Loading a previously saved model is easy:

A. Load the entire model

```
loaded_model = keras.models.load_model("fashion_model.h5")
```

Now you can evaluate or predict instantly:

```
loaded_model.evaluate(x_test, y_test)
loaded_model.predict(some_input)
```

B. Load only weights

```
model.load_weights("fashion_weights.h5")
```

Note:

The architecture **must match exactly** when loading weights only.

10.8 Summary

- ✓ Deep learning models are built from layers of neurons organized into different architectures like feedforward networks, CNNs, RNNs, and Transformers.
- ✓ Layers, epochs, batches, and hyperparameters control how a neural network learns and how well it performs.
- ✓ Loss functions measure how far predictions are from the true values, while optimizers adjust the model's weights to reduce that error.
- ✓ Activation functions such as ReLU, Sigmoid, and Softmax give neural networks the ability to learn complex, non-linear patterns.
- ✓ Model evaluation uses tools like training/validation splits, accuracy, confusion matrices, and loss curves to measure real performance.
- ✓ The Fashion MNIST project demonstrates how to build, train, evaluate, and make predictions with a deep neural network using Keras.
- ✓ Keras makes it easy to save and load trained models so they can be reused without retraining.

Chapter 11:
Advanced Neural Network Architectures

11.1 Convolutional Neural Networks (CNNs)

Traditional neural networks work well for simple tasks, but they struggle when dealing with images. Images are high-dimensional, contain spatial structure, and require models to detect patterns like edges, textures, shapes, and objects. This is exactly why **Convolutional Neural Networks (CNNs)** were created.

CNNs are deep learning models designed specifically for **computer vision** tasks such as:

- Image classification
- Object detection
- Facial recognition
- Medical imaging
- Self-driving car perception

Unlike fully connected networks, CNNs can automatically detect important visual patterns without needing manual feature engineering.

Why CNNs Work Better for Images

- Instead of looking at the entire image at once, CNNs focus on small regions (like 3×3 or 5×5 pixel areas). This mimics how humans see — your eyes process small patches and combine them into a full picture.
- CNNs use filters (also called kernels) that slide across the image to detect Edges, Corners and Patterns.
- Early layers learn simple features (edges, lines). Deeper layers learn complex features (faces, shapes, objects).

This hierarchy allows CNNs to understand visual content extremely well.

11.2 Convolution, Pooling & Feature Extraction

Convolutional Neural Networks (CNNs) rely on three core concepts—**convolution**, **pooling**, and **feature extraction**. These operations allow CNNs to work efficiently with images by identifying important visual patterns while reducing unnecessary information.

Let's break these concepts down in simple terms.

1. Convolution Layers:

Convolution is the operation that gives CNNs their name. It involves sliding a small filter (also called a kernel) across an image and performing element-wise multiplication.

How It Works

- A filter (e.g., 3×3) scans the image, one small patch at a time.
- Each patch is multiplied with the filter.
- The results are summed to produce a single value.
- Repeating this across the whole image produces a **feature map**.

These filters are **learned** during training — not manually programmed.

2. Feature Maps:

As filters scan the image, they create new images called **feature maps**.

- Early layers detect low-level features (edges, curves)
- Middle layers detect patterns (eyes, wheels, textures)
- Deep layers detect whole objects (faces, cats, cars)

This hierarchy of features is what makes CNNs so powerful for vision tasks.

3. Pooling Layers:

Pooling reduces the size of feature maps while keeping important information intact. It makes the model faster, more efficient, and less sensitive to small changes in the input. Benefits of Pooling are:

- Reduces image size → fewer computations
- Prevents overfitting
- Keeps only the strongest features
- Makes CNNs scale to large images

4. Convolution + Pooling = Feature Extraction

By combining convolution and pooling layers, CNNs automatically learn:

- What features matter
- Where they appear
- How important they are

✓ ***This eliminates the need for manual feature engineering that traditional ML models require.***

A basic CNN structure looks like this:

```
Input Image
   ↓
Convolution Layer
   ↓
Activation (ReLU)
   ↓
Pooling Layer
   ↓
Convolution Layer
   ↓
Pooling Layer
   ↓
Flatten Layer
   ↓
Dense (Fully Connected) Layers
   ↓
Output Layer
```

This pipeline turns raw pixels into meaningful patterns, which are then used for final classification.

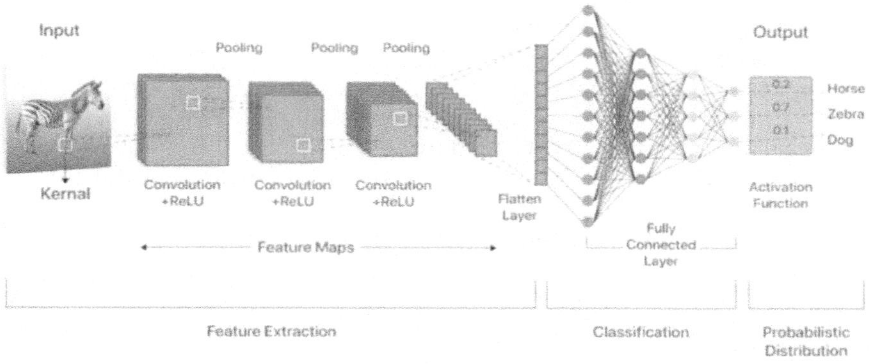

11.3 Hands-On: Image Classification with a CNN

Now that you understand how convolution and pooling work, it's time to build your first **Convolutional Neural Network (CNN)** in Keras. In this project, you'll train a CNN on the **CIFAR-10** dataset — a popular dataset of 60,000 small images across 10 categories such as airplanes, cars, birds, cats, and dogs.

Compared to MNIST and Fashion-MNIST, CIFAR-10 is more challenging because:

- Images are colored (RGB)
- Resolution is larger (32×32 pixels)
- Categories are more complex

This makes it a perfect dataset to learn how CNNs perform in real computer vision tasks.

Python Code: *Image Classification with a CNN*

```
# Step 1: Import libraries
import tensorflow as tf
from tensorflow import keras
from tensorflow.keras import layers
from tensorflow.keras.datasets import cifar10

# Step 2: Load the CIFAR-10 dataset
(x_train, y_train), (x_test, y_test) = cifar10.load_data()

# Step 3: Normalize pixel values (0-255 → 0-1)
x_train = x_train / 255.0
x_test = x_test / 255.0
```

```
# Step 4: Build the CNN model
model = keras.Sequential([
    layers.Conv2D(
    32, (3,3), activation='relu',  input_shape=(32, 32, 3)),
    layers.MaxPooling2D((2,2)),

    layers.Conv2D(64, (3,3), activation='relu'),
    layers.MaxPooling2D((2,2)),

    layers.Conv2D(64, (3,3), activation='relu'),

    layers.Flatten(),
    layers.Dense(64, activation='relu'),
    layers.Dense(10, activation='softmax')  # 10 classes
])

# Step 5: Compile the model
model.compile(
    optimizer='adam',
    loss='sparse_categorical_crossentropy',
    metrics=['accuracy']
)

# Step 6: Train the model
history = model.fit(
    x_train, y_train,
    epochs=10,
    batch_size=64,
    validation_split=0.2
)

# Step 7: Evaluate the model
test_loss, test_acc = model.evaluate(x_test, y_test)
print("Test accuracy:", test_acc)

# Step 8: Make predictions
predictions = model.predict(x_test)
print("Predicted class for first image:",
         tf.argmax(predictions[0]).numpy())
```

Expected Output

During training, you'll see accuracy improve steadily over 10 epochs:

```
Epoch 1/10
625/625 ━━━━━━━ 10s - accuracy: 0.55 - val_accuracy: 0.63
Epoch 5/10
625/625 ━━━━━━━ 8s  - accuracy: 0.74 - val_accuracy: 0.71
Epoch 10/10
625/625 ━━━━━━━ 8s  - accuracy: 0.80 - val_accuracy: 0.74
```

Typical test accuracy:

Test accuracy: 0.72 - 0.76

Achieving ~75% accuracy on CIFAR-10 with a small CNN is excellent and demonstrates how powerful convolutional layers are compared to dense networks alone.

What This Project Teaches You

- ✓ How to load and preprocess image datasets
- ✓ How to build a CNN using Conv2D and MaxPooling layers
- ✓ How CNNs extract visual features
- ✓ How to train, validate, and evaluate a vision model
- ✓ How deep learning handles real images beyond simple digits

This hands-on project lays the foundation for more advanced architecture work in the next sections.

11.4 Recurrent Neural Networks (RNNs)

While CNNs are excellent for images, many real-world problems involve **sequences** — data where order matters. For example:

- A sentence (words come in sequence)
- Audio/speech (sound varies over time)
- Stock prices (time series)
- Sensor readings (timestamps)
- DNA sequences

Traditional neural networks treat inputs independently and cannot capture **temporal patterns**. This is where **Recurrent Neural Networks (RNNs)** come in.

1. What Are RNNs?

Recurrent Neural Networks (RNN) are designed to handle sequential data by having a **memory** of previous inputs. They're the first major family of networks built to understand **order and context**, which is why they became so popular before **Transformers** arrived.

2. Why RNNs Are Good for Sequences

RNNs understand patterns such as:

- Word relationships in sentences
- Trends in time-series data
- Rising/falling patterns in stock prices
- Rhythm and structure in speech

They are the foundation of many sequence-based AI applications before Transformers became mainstream.

1. **Applications of RNNs**
    - **Natural Language Processing (NLP):**
      Text classification, sentiment analysis, named entity recognition.
    - **Speech Recognition:**
      Converting spoken words into text by processing audio sequences.
    - **Machine Translation:**
      Translating text from one language to another.
    - **Time-Series Prediction:**
      Stock price forecasting, weather modeling.
    - **Music Generation:**
      Predicting the next note based on previous notes.

4. Limitations of Simple RNNs

Basic RNNs struggle with:

- Long-term dependencies (remembering information far back)
- Vanishing gradients (gradients shrink during backpropagation)
- Slow training

These challenges led to the creation of improved architecture **Transformers** which solve most of these issues.

11.5 When to Use CNNs vs RNNs

Choosing the right neural network architecture depends primarily on the **type and structure of the data**, not on model complexity. Convolutional Neural Networks (CNNs) and Recurrent Neural Networks (RNNs) are designed to solve different kinds of problems, and understanding when to use each is an important practical skill.

Convolutional Neural Networks (CNNs) are best suited for data that has a **spatial structure**, where relationships between nearby elements matter. Images are the most common example, as neighboring pixels often contain related information. CNNs use convolutional filters to automatically detect local patterns such as edges, textures, and shapes, and then combine these patterns into higher-level features.

Typical use cases for CNNs include image classification, object detection, facial recognition, and medical image analysis.

Recurrent Neural Networks (RNNs) are designed for **sequential data**, where the order of elements is important and past information influences future predictions. RNNs maintain an internal state (or memory) that allows them to process data step by step, making them well suited for tasks involving time or sequence dependencies. Common applications of RNNs include time series forecasting, speech recognition, text processing, and sequence-based prediction tasks.

In practice, the choice between CNNs and RNNs can be summarized as follows:

- Use **CNNs** when working with images or grid-like data where spatial relationships are important.
- Use **RNNs** when working with ordered sequences where context and timing matter.

It is also worth noting that modern deep learning systems often **combine architectures**. For example, CNNs may be used to extract features from images, while RNNs or other sequence models process those features over time. As you move further into deep learning, you will also encounter **Transformer-based models**, which extend these ideas and handle both spatial and sequential patterns efficiently.

Understanding these distinctions will help you select appropriate architectures and build more effective deep learning solutions.

11.6 Summary

In this chapter, you explored **advanced neural network architectures** and learned how different designs are suited to different types of data. Rather than relying on a single model type, modern deep learning systems use specialized architectures to handle images, sequences, and structured patterns effectively.

You gained an understanding of how **Convolutional Neural Networks (CNNs)** are used for spatial data such as images, and how **Recurrent Neural Networks (RNNs)** are applied to sequential data where order and context matter. More importantly, you learned how to choose between architectures based on the nature of the problem, not just model complexity.

With this architectural foundation in place, you are now prepared to move into the next part of the book, where deep learning techniques are extended to **Generative AI, Large Language Models, and Agentic AI**—systems that can generate content, reason over information, and act autonomously.

Part IV – Agentic AI, Generative AI & Large Language Models

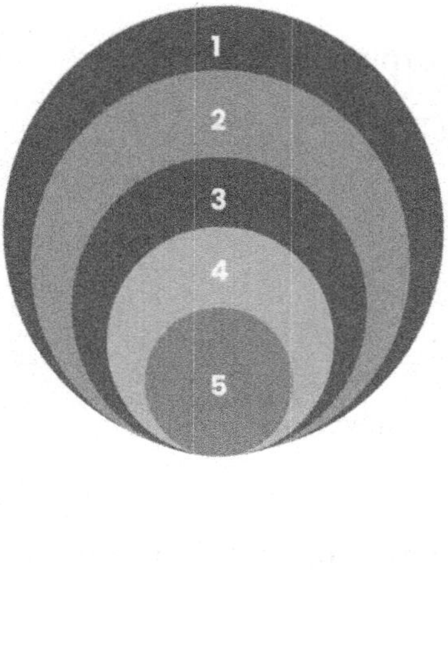

1 Artifical Intelligence

A broad term encompassing the development and use of computer systems capable of performing tasks that typically require human intelligence.

2 Machine Learning

A subset of AI that trains systems to learn from data and make decisions or predictions based on patterns.

3 Neural Networks

A type of machine learning algorithm that mimics the structure and function of the human brain—allowing AI systems to learn and process complex data.

4 Deep Learning

A subfield of machine learning that uses neural networks with multiple layers to learn and extract features from data.

5 Generative AI

A subset of AI that focuses on generating new content, such as text or images, based on patterns learned from data.

Chapter 12:
Generative AI & Autoencoders

12.1 What Is Generative AI?

Generative AI refers to a class of artificial intelligence models that can **create new content** — such as images, text, audio, video, designs, and even code. Unlike traditional AI systems that simply classify or predict, generative AI models can produce completely new outputs that have never existed before.

This technology is behind many cutting-edge applications today:

- Image generation tools (Midjourney, DALL·E)
- Large language models (ChatGPT, GPT-4/5)
- Synthetic voices and music
- Video generation
- Style transfer and creative design
- Drug discovery and molecule generation

Generative AI does not just recognize patterns — it **learns the distribution** of data and then **creates new samples** that resemble the originals.

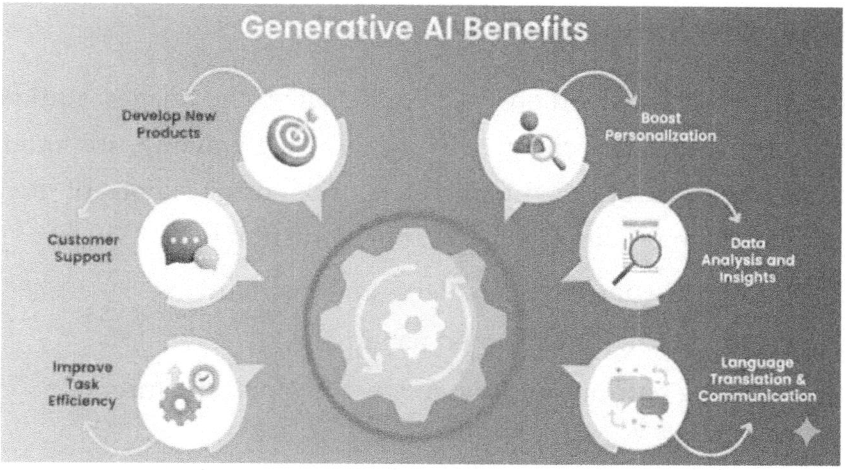

GenAI Features and Capabilities:

Generative AI development comes with a host of impressive features:

- **Creates New Content:** It can generate text, images, music, and even entire videos from scratch.
- **Learns Patterns:** By analyzing large amounts of data, it understands patterns and structures, which it then uses to create new outputs.
- **Adapts to Different Tasks:** Whether it's writing a poem, designing a product, or developing a new recipe, generative AI can adapt to various tasks.
- **Improves Over Time:** The more data it processes, the better it becomes at creating new content. It continuously learns and refines its abilities.

How Generative AI Works:

Generative AI is trained on large datasets like text, images, audio or video using deep learning networks. During training, the model learns from dataset called parameters (millions or billions of them) that help them predict or generate new content by:

1. Learning the underlying patterns and distributions
2. Sampling from those learned patterns
3. Producing new outputs that follow the same structure

Different **generative models** achieve this in different ways, such as:

- **Autoencoders** (compress + reconstruct)
- **GANs** (two networks competing)
- **Diffusion models** (denoise images step by step, used in DALL·E 3, Midjourney)
- **Transformers** (predict the next token to generate text/images/audio)

Applications of Generative AI:

Generative AI powers applications across industries:

- **Text:** Powers chatbots, virtual assistants, content creation, document summarization and even code generation tools like GitHub Copilot.
- **Images:** Used in digital art, product design, fashion, advertising and medical imaging to create visuals that are close to real-world examples.
- **Audio & Speech:** Enables natural-sounding voice assistants, multilingual dubbing, music composition, personalized voice cloning and accessibility tools.

- **Video:** Supports animation, movie special effects, gaming, marketing videos and realistic training simulations.
- **Business Use Cases:** Enhances customer support with AI agents, boosts knowledge discovery, accelerates drug discovery, assists in financial forecasting and improves data-driven decision-making.

Generative models have opened the door to entirely new workflows and tools that were impossible just a few years ago.

12.2 Discriminative vs. Generative Models

Before diving deeper into GenAI models, it's important to understand the difference between **discriminative** and **generative** models. These are the two major categories of machine learning approaches, and each solves a fundamentally different type of problem.

1. What Are Discriminative Models?

Discriminative models learn to **distinguish** between different classes. They model the boundary between categories.
In simple terms:

Discriminative models answer: "Given X, what is Y?"

Examples:

- Given an image (X), is it a cat or a dog? (Y)
- Given text (X), is the sentiment positive or negative? (Y)

These models focus only on predicting labels.
They learn:

$P(Y \mid X) \rightarrow$ the probability of a label Y given the input X

Examples of Discriminative Models:

In our book we discussed most of the following Models in previous chapters.

- Logistic Regression
- Decision Trees
- Random Forest
- SVM
- CNNs (for classification)
- LSTMs (for sentiment analysis)

Discriminative models are excellent for prediction tasks but **cannot generate new data**.

2. What Are Generative Models?

Generative models learn the **underlying distribution** of the data itself.
Instead of just predicting labels, they understand how data is structured.

Generative models answer: "Given Y, what does X look like?"
Or even: "Generate a new X from scratch."
They can create:

- New images
- New sentences
- New audio
- New designs
- New data samples

They learn:

$P(X \mid Y)$ → the probability of data X belonging to class Y

$P(X)$ → the distribution of the data itself

Examples of Generative Models

- Autoencoders
- GANs
- Diffusion Models (used in DALL·E 3, Midjourney, Stable Diffusion)
- Large Language Models (GPT, LLaMA, Claude)

Generative models are responsible for modern AI creativity and synthesis.

3. Key Differences (Simple Comparison)

Feature	Discriminative Models	Generative Models
Goal	Predict labels	Create new data
Learn	Boundary between classes	Data distribution
Answers	"What class is this?"	"What does this class look like?"
Output	Labels, probabilities	Images, text, audio, samples
Examples	CNNs, Logistic Regression	GANs, VAEs, GPT

In summary:

- Discriminative models → classify
- Generative models → create

12.3 Autoencoders

Autoencoders are one of the foundational building blocks of generative AI. They learn to **compress data into a smaller representation** and then **reconstruct it**, capturing important patterns in the process.

What Is an Autoencoder?

An autoencoder is a neural network trained to **reconstruct its own input**. It consists of two parts:

Encoder: Compresses the input into a smaller representation called the **latent vector** or **latent space**.

Decoder: Reconstructs the original input from the latent vector.

```
Input → [Encoder] → Latent Space → [Decoder] → Output
(The Output is Reconstructed Input)
```

The goal during training: **Make the output look as close as possible to the input.**

What Autoencoders Learn:

Autoencoders learn:

- Structure
- Important features
- Patterns
- Compressed representations

They are often used for:

- Image compression
- Noise removal (Denoising Autoencoders)
- Dimensionality reduction
- Feature extraction
- Data visualization

12.4 GANs: Generative Adversarial Networks

Generative Adversarial Networks (GANs) are one of the most groundbreaking inventions in deep learning.

A **Generative Adversarial Network (GAN)** is a **Generative AI** model that uses two competing neural networks—a generator and a discriminator—to create new, realistic data. It can generate **incredibly realistic images**, audio, and even videos — often indistinguishable from real examples.

GANs power technologies like:

- AI-generated artwork
- Deepfake videos
- Synthetic human faces (This Person Does Not Exist)
- Super-resolution imaging
- Image-to-image translation (e.g., turning sketches into photos)

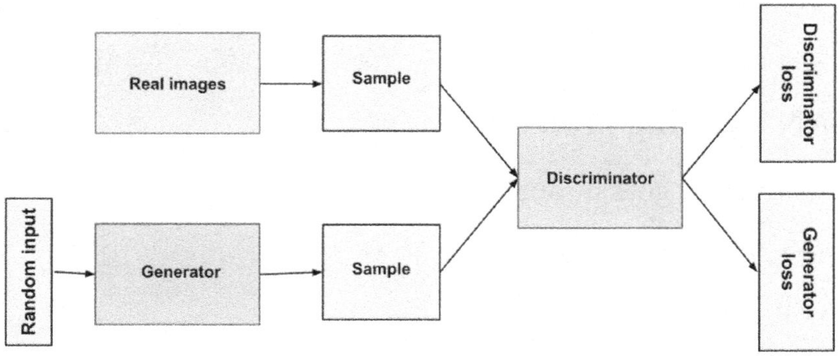

Let's explore how they work in simple terms.

How GAN's Work:

A GAN is made of **two neural networks**:

The Generator (G):

- Takes random noise as input
- Tries to create **fake samples** that look real
- Its goal: *fool the discriminator*

The Discriminator (D):

- Takes an image (real or fake)
- Tries to classify it correctly
- Its goal: *detect fakes*

They play a **cat-and-mouse game**:

```
Generator → produces fake images
Discriminator → tries to detect them
```

Over time:

- The **Generator gets better** at creating realistic images
- The **Discriminator gets better** at spotting fakes

This competitive training leads to extremely high-quality outputs.

GAN Training Process:

GAN training goes through a repeated cycle:

Step 1: Train the Discriminator:

Give it:

- Real images (label = 1)
- Fake images from the Generator (label = 0)

It learns to detect real vs fake.

Step 2: Train the Generator:

Freeze the discriminator's weights.

- Give the generator random noise → generate fake images.
- Pass those images to the discriminator, but set the label as real (1).

The generator improves by making images that fool the discriminator. This back-and-forth loop continues until:

- The generator produces images so realistic that…
- The discriminator struggles to tell real from fake.

3. What Makes GANs Special?

GANs are unique because:

- They **learn without labeled data**
- They produce **sharp, detailed images**
- They can model complex distributions
- They enable many creative tasks

GANs have become a core part of generative AI research.

12.5 Hands-On Project: Image Generation with a GAN

In this project, you will build a **simple Generative Adversarial Network (GAN)** using Keras. The GAN will learn to generate new digit-like images similar to MNIST handwritten digits (0–9).

Project Goal:

The goal is to train a basic GAN on the MNIST handwritten digits dataset to generate **new images of digits** using only random noise as input.

Python Code: Image Generation with a GAN

```
# Import libraries
import tensorflow as tf
from tensorflow import keras
from tensorflow.keras import layers
import numpy as np

# Load and prepare MNIST (only images)
(x_train, _), _ = keras.datasets.mnist.load_data()
x_train = x_train.astype("float32") / 255.0
x_train = x_train.reshape(-1, 28 * 28) # flatten to vectors

latent_dim = 100  # size of random noise vector

# Generator: noise (100) -> fake image (784)
generator = keras.Sequential([
    layers.Input(shape=(latent_dim,)),
    layers.Dense(128, activation="relu"),
    layers.Dense(28 * 28, activation="sigmoid")
])

# Discriminator: image (784) -> real/fake (1)
discriminator = keras.Sequential([
    layers.Input(shape=(28 * 28,)),
    layers.Dense(128, activation="relu"),
    layers.Dense(1, activation="sigmoid")
])
discriminator.compile(optimizer="adam",
                      loss="binary_crossentropy")

# GAN: noise -> generator -> discriminator
discriminator.trainable = False  # freeze inside GAN
gan_input = keras.Input(shape=(latent_dim,))
gan_output = discriminator(generator(gan_input))
gan = keras.Model(gan_input, gan_output)
gan.compile(optimizer="adam", loss="binary_crossentropy")

batch_size = 128
epochs = 3000

for epoch in range(epochs):
    # 1) Train discriminator
    noise = np.random.normal(0, 1, size=(batch_size,  latent_dim))
    fake_images = generator.predict(noise, verbose=0)
    idx = np.random.randint(0, x_train.shape[0], batch_size)
```

```
real_images = x_train[idx]
x = np.vstack([real_images, fake_images])
y = np.vstack([np.ones((batch_size, 1)),
               np.zeros((batch_size, 1))])
d_loss = discriminator.train_on_batch(x, y)

# 2) Train generator (through GAN)
noise = np.random.normal(0,1,size=(batch_size, latent_dim))
# y_gen generator to fool discriminator
y_gen = np.ones((batch_size, 1))
g_loss = gan.train_on_batch(noise, y_gen)

if epoch % 500 == 0:
  print(f"Epoch {epoch} | D loss: {d_loss:.4f} | G loss:
        {g_loss:.4f}")
```

Expected Output

```
During training, you will see logs like:
Epoch 0 | D loss: 0.5687 | G loss: 0.9965
Epoch 500 | D loss: 3.5393 | G loss: 0.0113
Epoch 1000 | D loss: 3.9356 | G loss: 0.0059
...
```

After around **3,000 training steps**, generated images begin to resemble digits. You can visualize generated samples with:

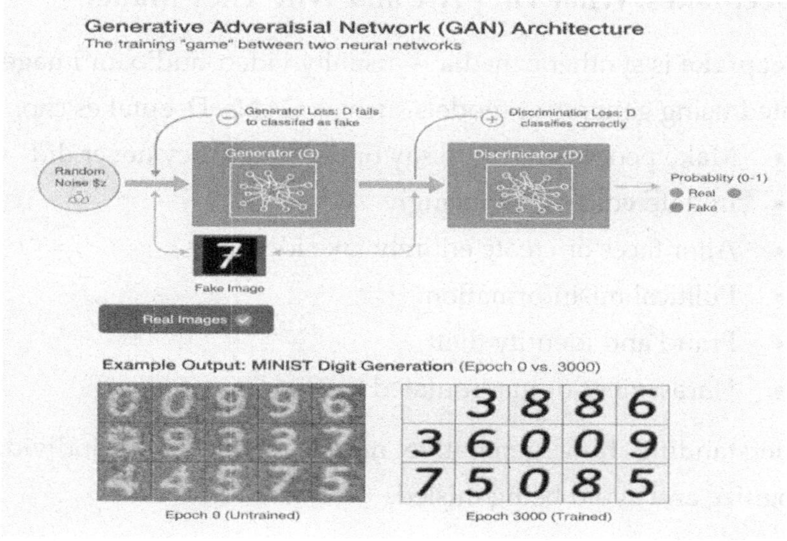

What This Project Teaches You:

- ✓ How to build a **Generator** network that creates images
- ✓ How to build a **Discriminator** that detects real vs fake
- ✓ How GANs learn through adversarial training
- ✓ How to generate synthetic images from random noise
- ✓ How to tune GAN training loops

12.6 Ethical Considerations and Deepfake Awareness

Generative AI is powerful, creative, and transformative — but it also introduces important ethical challenges. As models become capable of producing realistic images, videos, and text, responsible use and awareness become essential. In this section, you'll learn the key risks and ethical considerations surrounding generative AI.

1. Deepfakes: What They Are and Why They Matter

A **deepfake** is synthetic media — usually video, audio, or images — created using generative models such as GANs. Deepfakes can:

- Make people appear to say or do things they never did
- Imitate voices convincingly
- Alter faces or create entirely fake identities
- Political misinformation
- Fraud and identity theft
- Harassment or manipulated media

Understanding how generative models work helps individuals recognize and avoid being misled.

2. Risks of Generative AI

Generative AI introduces several risks:

- **Misinformation & Manipulation:** Fake images or videos can spread rapidly, influencing public opinion.
- **Privacy Concerns:** Models trained on public images may unintentionally reproduce private or copyrighted content.
- **Bias in Generated Content:** If training data contains biases, generated content may reinforce harmful stereotypes.
- **Security Threats:** Fake voices or documents can be used for fraud and identity theft.
- **Ethical Use in Sensitive Fields:** Medical or financial synthetic data must be clearly labeled and validated.

3. Responsible Use Guidelines

To use generative AI ethically, consider these best practices:

- **Be Transparent:** Label AI-generated content whenever possible.
- **Obtain Consent:** Avoid using real people's faces, voices, or personal data without permission.
- **Avoid Harmful Use Cases:** Do not generate misleading or harmful content.
- **Check for Bias:** Evaluate generative outputs for fairness and unintended bias.
- **Use AI Detection Tools:** Tools can help identify deepfakes or AI-generated text/images.
- **Follow Legal and Platform Policies:** Different countries and online platforms have regulations regarding synthetic media.

4. Positive Uses of Generative AI

Despite risks, generative AI also has many ethical and beneficial uses:

- Assistive creativity for designers and artists
- Generating synthetic training data for medical or scientific research
- Restoring old or damaged photos
- Creating realistic simulations for robotics
- Enhancing video games and virtual worlds
- Helping writers and developers with ideation

The key is ensuring the technology is used responsibly and transparently.

5. How to Stay Informed

Generative AI evolves rapidly. To stay safe and aware:

✓ Learn how deepfakes are made and detected

✓ Follow AI ethics guidelines from credible organizations

✓ Keep up with new regulations around synthetic media

✓ Use watermarking and authenticity tools where available

Being informed helps protect against misuse and promotes responsible innovation.

12.7 Summary

In this chapter, you explored the foundations of **Generative AI** and how generative models differ from traditional predictive approaches. You learned how models such as **autoencoders** and **Generative Adversarial Networks (GANs)** can learn data representations and generate new content based on learned patterns.

You also examined ethical considerations surrounding generative technologies, including the risks of misuse and deepfakes. With these concepts in place, you are now prepared to move on to **Large Language Models and prompt engineering**, where generative AI is applied at scale to natural language tasks.

Chapter 13:
Large Language Models & Prompt Engineering

13.1 Transformers: The NLP Revolution

Natural Language Processing (NLP) has gone through several major breakthroughs over the past decade. Each step brought us closer to the advanced Large Language Models (LLMs) we use today — models capable of writing essays, generating code, answering questions, and holding natural conversations.

This section explains how we moved from simple sequence models to the transformer architecture that powers modern AI systems.

1. The Early Days: RNNs and LSTMs

Before transformers, most NLP models were built using **Recurrent Neural Networks (RNNs)** and **Long Short-Term Memory networks (LSTMs)**.

Strengths of RNNs/LSTMs

- Good at handling sequential data
- Able to capture short-term context

- Widely used for translation, speech processing, and sentiment analysis

Limitations

- Slow to train because they process one word at a time
- Difficult to parallelize on modern hardware
- Struggled with long sentences
- Long-term dependencies often lost due to vanishing gradients

These limitations created the need for a new, more scalable architecture.

2. What are Transformers

In 2017, Google introduced the paper **"Attention Is All You Need,"** which described the **transformer** architecture. They are meant to solve any task that transforms an input sequence to an output sequence. This is why they are called "**Transformers**".

A transformer is a type of artificial intelligence model that learns to understand and generate human-like text by analyzing patterns in large amounts of text data.

Transformers removed the need for recurrence entirely and replaced it with a mechanism called **self-attention**, allowing models to:

- Understand relationships between all words simultaneously
- Train significantly faster
- Scale to massive sizes
- Capture long-range dependencies with ease

This breakthrough sparked the modern NLP revolution.

3. Why Transformers Changed Everything

Transformers solved many long-standing NLP challenges:

1. Parallel Processing: They process entire sequences at once rather than word by word, making training dramatically faster.

2. Long-Range Understanding: Self-attention lets them connect words across long distances:
Example:
"The cat that chased the mouse **was hungry**."
The model learns that **cat** ↔ **was hungry**, even across multiple words.

3. Scalability: Transformers improve significantly as they increase in size (from millions to billions and trillions of parameters). This scaling effect enabled powerful LLMs such as GPT-4, GPT-5, LLaMA, Gemini, and Claude.

4. Universal Architecture: Transformers now power:

- Language models
- Image processing systems
- Audio understanding
- Multimodal AI (text + images + audio)

4. The Birth of Large Language Models (LLMs)

As transformers matured, researchers began training increasingly large models:

- **GPT (2018)** → first major transformer-based generator
- **BERT (2019)** → bidirectional language understanding
- **GPT-3 (2020)** → major leap in generative capability
- **ChatGPT (2022)** → conversational, aligned LLM
- **GPT-5, LLaMA, Claude, Gemini** → advanced reasoning + multimodal abilities

These models are trained on **trillions of words** and can:

✓ Write essays
✓ Generate code
✓ Answer questions
✓ Translate languages
✓ Understand context and nuance

This development laid the foundation for today's AI revolution.

13.2 How Attention and Self-Attention Work

The breakthrough that made transformers possible — and enabled modern Large Language Models — is the **attention mechanism**, especially **self-attention**. This concept allows a model to understand which words in a sentence are important relative to each other, no matter how far apart they are.

This section explains attention in simple terms so you can fully grasp how transformers think.

1. What Is Attention?

Attention lets a model decide:

"How much should I focus on each word when processing the current word?"

For each word, the model looks at *all* the other words and assigns importance scores.

Example sentence:

"The cat that chased the mouse **was hungry**."

When processing **cat**, the model notices:

"cat" relates strongly to "was hungry"

Less to "chased"

Even less to "mouse"

This leads to a weighted understanding of the sentence.

2. What Is Self-Attention?

Self-attention is attention applied **within the same sequence**. Every word attends to every other word — including itself.

This means the model creates a network of relationships:

cat ↔ chased

cat ↔ mouse

cat ↔ was hungry

mouse ↔ chased

mouse ↔ was

The model builds a complete contextual map of the sentence.

3. How Self-Attention Works (Simple Mechanics)

Each word is transformed into three vectors:

Q — Query: What the word is looking for.

K — Key: What the word offers in context.

V — Value: The actual information the word carries.

Then the model computes: Attention Score = Q · K

This score shows how important each word is to every other word.

Finally: `Output = Σ (Attention Score × V)`

This allows the model to combine information from all words in proportion to their relevance.

Self-Attention Example:

Sentence: "I saw the man with a telescope."

Self-attention helps the model understand both interpretations:

- "I used a telescope to see the man."
- "The man had a telescope."

The **model learns context** through multiple attention heads.

4. Why This Matters

Self-attention is the heart of transformers. It enables:

- GPT-style text generation
- BERT-style text understanding
- Multimodal models

Without attention, large language models would not be possible.

Next, we'll explore how major transformer architectures like **GPT**, **BERT**, and **T5** are structured.

13.3 Large Language Model Architectural Overview

Transformers introduced a new approach to language processing, and today's most advanced AI systems are built on three major architectural families: **GPT**, **BERT/Gemini-style encoders**, and **modern large-scale transformer hybrids**. Each serves a different purpose—generation, understanding, or both.

This section provides a clear overview of how these models work and how their designs differ

1. The Transformer Architecture

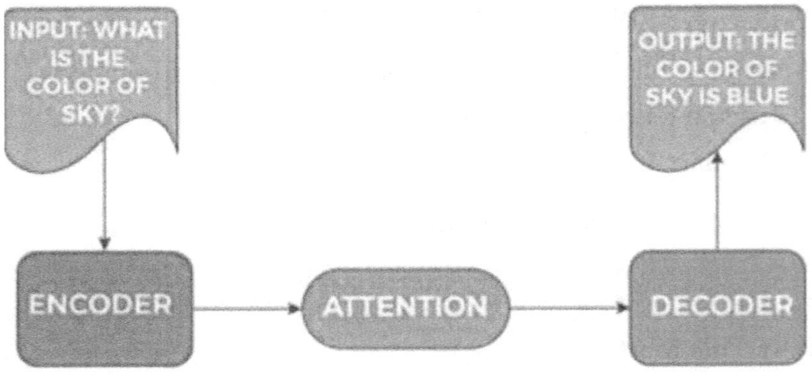

Large Language Models (LLMs) are built on the **Transformer** architecture, which consists of two main components:

- **Encoder** — processes and understands input
- **Decoder** — generates output

The **Encoder** functions as the model's reader. It processes the entire input sequence at once, learning the relationships between words and producing a contextual representation.

The **Decoder** acts as the generator, producing text one token at a time based on the encoder's representations and its own previously generated tokens.

Different models use different parts of this architecture:

- Some use **only the encoder**
- Some use **only the decoder**
- Some use **both** in combination

2. BERT: Encoder-Only Model (Understands Language)

BERT (Bidirectional Encoder Representations from Transformers) uses only the encoder stack and is optimized for understanding tasks.

Strengths:

- Sentence understanding
- Text classification
- Entity extraction
- Question answering
- Sentiment analysis

Key Features:

- Bidirectional attention (looks left and right simultaneously)
- Masked language modeling
- Strong performance on comprehension tasks

Common Use Cases:

- Spam detection
- Document classification
- Search relevance
- Chatbot intent detection

3. GPT: Decoder-Only Model (Generates Language)

GPT (Generative Pre-trained Transformer) uses only the decoder side of the transformer and excels at text generation.

Strengths:

- Human-like text generation
- Story writing and content creation
- Coding assistance
- Translation
- Conversational AI

Key Features:

- Autoregressive next-token prediction
- Trained to complete sequences
- Excellent scaling performance
- Forms the basis of GPT-3, GPT-4, GPT-5 and ChatGPT

Use Cases:

- Chat interfaces and Code generation
- Writing assistants
- AI reasoning tools

4. Encoder-Decoder Models: T5, FLAN-T5, and More

Encoder–decoder models combine both components, making them highly versatile. E.g. **T5 (Text-to-Text Transfer Transformer).**

Treats every task as a text-to-text problem:

- Input: "Translate English to French: Hello"
- Output: "Bonjour"

Strengths: Works for translation, summarization, classification, and Q&A. General-purpose and easy to fine-tune

5. Modern LLM Families

Modern LLMs extend these architectures at massive scale:

GPT-4, GPT-5

- Decoder-only
- Trained on trillions of tokens
- Strong reasoning, coding, and conversational abilities

LLaMA, Falcon, Mistral

- Efficient decoder-only architectures
- Popular open-source models

Claude, Gemini

- Hybrid architectures with advanced training methods
- Multimodal capabilities (text, image, audio)
- Optimized for reasoning and safety

6. How These Models Differ

Model	Architecture	Strength
BERT	Encoder-only	Understanding language
GPT	Decoder-only	Generating language
T5	Encoder–decoder	Translating or transforming text
LLaMA / Mistral	Decoder-only	Efficient open-source LLMs
GPT-5 / Gemini / Claude	Hybrid	Reasoning, multimodal, high performance

7. Why This Matters

Understanding these architectures helps you:

- Choose the right model for your application
- Understand how GPT-style models generate text
- Fine-tune transformer models effectively
- Build AI applications on modern LLM foundations
- Better appreciate how systems like ChatGPT operate internally

This sets the stage for the next section, where we explore how LLMs are trained: tokenization, pre-training, fine-tuning, and alignment.

13.4 How LLMs Are Trained and Fine-Tuned

Large Language Models (LLMs) such as GPT-5, Claude, LLaMA, and Gemini go through a multi-stage training process. Each stage teaches the model something different — from basic language patterns to advanced reasoning and safe interactions. Understanding these stages is essential for knowing how LLMs work and how they can be adapted for specific tasks.

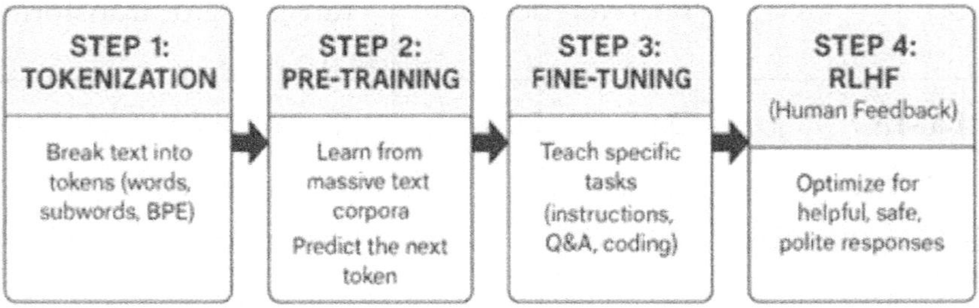

Step 1: Tokenization — Breaking Text Into Pieces:

Before training begins, all text is broken into **tokens**. Tokens may be:

- Words
- Subwords
- Characters
- Byte-pair encodings (BPE)

Example tokenization:

```
Input: "ChatGPT is amazing!"
Output: ["Chat", "G", "PT", " is", " amazing", "!"]
```

LLMs learn patterns **at the token level**, not the word level.

Step 2: Pre-Training — Learning From Massive Text Corpora:

Pre-training is the biggest and most expensive stage. The model learns by predicting the **next token** in a sequence. E.g.

```
Input: "The cat sat on the ___"
Output: "The cat sat on the wall"
```

This is called **autoregressive training**.

During pre-training, the model learns:

- Grammar, vocabulary, world knowledge
- Reasoning patterns, Logic, writing styles

Data Sources Include:

- Books, Websites, Articles
- Code repositories, public forums, synthetic data

The dataset usually contains **trillions of tokens**.

Goal: Teach the model to understand and generate human-like language.

Step 3: Fine-Tuning — Teaching the Model Specific Tasks:

After pre-training, the model is very knowledgeable but not task-optimized.

Fine-tuning teaches it:

- How to follow instructions. How to answer questions
- How to translate. How to summarize
- How to code

This is done by training on curated, labeled datasets:

```
Input: "Summarize this article"
Output: "The article explains…"
```

Fine-tuning makes the model more useful for real applications.

Step 4: Reinforcement Learning from Human Feedback (RLHF)

RLHF is what made tools like ChatGPT friendly, safe, and conversational.

Humans rate model responses:

- "Good answer"; "Bad answer"; "Unsafe answer"
- "Helpful"; "Harmless"; "Honest"

The model is then optimized to produce the *preferred* response using reinforcement learning (often PPO).

RLHF teaches the model:

- To follow instructions
- To avoid harmful content
- To sound polite and helpful
- To reason step-by-step
- To reject dangerous requests

This is why tools like ChatGPT feel conversational and aligned with human preferences.

Step 5: Safety Training & Guardrails

Modern models go through additional safety steps:

- Filtering harmful content
- Training with safety-specific datasets
- Red-teaming (testing against harmful prompts)
- Adding refusal mechanisms

This ensures safer use in real-world environments.

Summary: This multilayered process is what transforms raw text data into **powerful language models** capable of reasoning, writing, summarizing, and assisting with complex tasks.

13.5 Prompt Engineering: Techniques and Best Practices

Prompt engineering is the practice of designing effective instructions that guide a Large Language Model (LLM) to produce accurate, useful, and reliable outputs. Although LLMs are powerful, their performance depends greatly on how questions, tasks, and constraints are expressed. A well-crafted prompt can improve reasoning quality, reduce errors, and make responses more aligned with the user's intent.

At its core, prompt engineering involves understanding how models interpret input patterns and how different styles of prompting influence the model's behavior. Good prompts help the model focus on the right context, clarify expectations, and adapt its response format to the task—whether it's answering a question, generating code, summarizing text, or creating structured data.

Key Principles of Prompt Engineering:

Effective prompting often relies on several strategies, such as:

- **Clear instructions**: State exactly what you want the model to do.
- **Providing context**: Include relevant information the model needs to answer correctly.
- **Specifying output format**: Define whether the answer should be a paragraph, list, JSON object, table, or something else.
- **Giving examples**: Use few-shot prompts (input–output pairs) to demonstrate the task.
- **Constraining behavior**: Set boundaries such as "use simple language" or "explain step-by-step."
- **Iterative refinement**: Adjust prompts based on the model's initial output to reach the desired result.

Types of Prompts:

Different prompt styles are useful for different tasks:

- **Instruction prompts**: "Explain how neural networks work in simple terms."
- **Contextual prompts**: Providing background before asking a question.
- **Chain-of-thought prompts**: Encouraging step-by-step reasoning, e.g., "Think through this problem carefully before answering."
- **Few-shot prompts**: Supplying examples to guide the model.
- **Role-based prompts**: Asking the model to act as a tutor, developer, analyst, or reviewer.
- **Constraint-based prompts**: Defining specific rules, limits, or formats.

Why Prompt Engineering Matters

Even though LLMs have strong general capabilities, their output quality varies depending on how tasks are phrased. Prompt engineering enables:

- More accurate and consistent results
- Better reasoning and problem-solving
- Reduced hallucinations and irrelevant outputs
- Higher-efficiency workflows for coding and writing tasks
- The ability to tailor the model's tone, structure, and behavior

Prompt engineering has become an essential skill for developers, analysts, and AI practitioners. As models evolve, prompting continues to play a crucial role in unlocking the full potential of LLMs.

13.6 Hands-On: Generate Text with a Pre-Trained GPT Model from Hugging Face

In this project, you will generate text (stories, paragraphs, explanations, etc.) using a pre-trained GPT-style language model. Instead of training a model from scratch, you will load an existing model and use it to complete prompts you provide.

This is exactly how many modern AI applications work behind the scenes: they send a prompt to a pre-trained model and return the generated text to the user.

What You'll Learn:

By the end of this project, you will be able to:

- Load a pre-trained GPT-style model in Python
- Generate text continuations from your own prompts
- Use prompting to get different kinds of outputs: stories, explanations, and more

1. Setup and Installation

You will use the **transformers library** from **Hugging Face**, which provides ready-to-use GPT-style models.

Note: This book uses Keras throughout most chapters. However, the Hugging Face Transformers library primarily supports PyTorch for modern GPT-style models, so the hands-on project in this chapter uses PyTorch.

Install the required packages:

```
pip install transformers torch
```

Note: The first time you run the code, the model will be downloaded from the Hugging Face. After that, it will be cached locally.

2. Load the GPT Model with PyTorch

In this example, you'll use **distilgpt2**, a small, fast version of GPT-2 that works well on a CPU.

```
from transformers import AutoTokenizer, AutoModelForCausalLM
import torch

model_name = "distilgpt2"

# tokenizer that converts text into tokens the model understands
tokenizer = AutoTokenizer.from_pretrained(model_name)

# Load the pre-trained GPT-style model for text generation
model = AutoModelForCausalLM.from_pretrained(model_name)
```

3. Create a Text Generation Function

This function takes a prompt, generates text, and returns the result.

```
def generate_text(prompt, max_new_tokens=50, temperature=0.7):
    # Convert input prompt to token IDs
    input_ids = tokenizer.encode(prompt, return_tensors="pt")

    # Generate new text using the GPT model
    output_ids = model.generate(
        input_ids,
        max_new_tokens=max_new_tokens,
        temperature=temperature,
        do_sample=True,        # enables randomness
        top_k=50,              # sample from top 50 tokens
        top_p=0.95,            # nucleus sampling
        eos_token_id=tokenizer.eos_token_id,
    )

   # Convert the generated token IDs back into text
   return tokenizer.decode(output_ids[0],skip_special_tokens=True)
```

Inside the generate_text function:

- **Encoding the prompt**
  The prompt string is first converted into a sequence of token IDs using the tokenizer. Models cannot process raw text, so every word must be transformed into numerical representations.

- **Generating text**
  The model's generate() function predicts new tokens that extend the prompt.
  - **max_new_tokens:** controls how long the continuation will be.
  - **temperature** adjusts randomness: lower values produce more focused text, while higher values produce more creative or unpredictable results.
  - **do_sample=True** enables sampling rather than choosing only the highest-probability token.

  - **top_k=50** restricts sampling to the top 50 most likely tokens.
  - **top_p=0.95** applies nucleus sampling, selecting tokens from the smallest group that makes up 95% of the probability distribution.

- **Decoding the output**
  Once the model generates token IDs, the tokenizer converts them back to readable text.

4. Generate Explanations on Prompt

Your GPT model can generate text on the prompt

```
prompt = "Explain what a neural network is in simple terms"
print(generate_text(prompt, max_new_tokens=80))
```

Another Example:

```
prompt = "Write why cybersecurity is important"
print(generate_text(prompt, max_new_tokens=80))
```

5. Experiment with Different Prompt Styles

Try prompts like:

- **Creative writing:** *"Write a science fiction story about humans living on Mars."*
- **Technical explanation:** *"Explain the difference between supervised and unsupervised learning."*
- **Business writing:** *"Write a professional email requesting a project update."*
- **Coding task:** *"Write a Python function that reverses a string."*

Encourage readers to try short, direct prompts — GPT models respond very strongly to the way tasks are phrased.

Complete Code Listing: Text Generation with a Pre-Trained GPT Model from Hugging Face

```
from transformers import AutoTokenizer, AutoModelForCausalLM
import torch

model_name = "distilgpt2"

# tokenizer that converts text into tokens the model understands
tokenizer = AutoTokenizer.from_pretrained(model_name)

# Load the pre-trained GPT-style model for text generation
model = AutoModelForCausalLM.from_pretrained(model_name)

def generate_text(prompt, max_new_tokens=50, temperature=0.7):
    # Convert input prompt to token IDs
    input_ids = tokenizer.encode(prompt, return_tensors="pt")

    # Generate new text using the GPT model
    output_ids = model.generate(
        input_ids,
        max_new_tokens=max_new_tokens,
        temperature=temperature,
        do_sample=True,        # enables randomness
        top_k=50,              # sample from top 50 tokens
        top_p=0.95,            # nucleus sampling
        eos_token_id=tokenizer.eos_token_id,
    )

   # Convert the generated token IDs back into text
   return tokenizer.decode(output_ids[0],skip_special_tokens=True)

prompt = "Explain what a neural network is in simple terms"
print(generate_text(prompt, max_new_tokens=80))

prompt = "Write why cybersecurity is important"
print(generate_text(prompt, max_new_tokens=80))
```

6. Summary of What You Accomplished

In this project, you:

- Loaded a GPT-style model using PyTorch
- Generated text from your own prompts
- Controlled the style and length of output
- Learned how prompting influences model behavior
- Experienced how LLMs serve as the engine behind AI applications

This project gives readers practical experience with **generation**, which is a core capability of modern LLMs.

13.7 Real-World Applications of Large Language Models

Large Language Models (LLMs) such as GPT-5, Gemini, Claude, LLaMA, and Mistral are transforming industries by enabling machines to understand and generate human language. Their ability to work with text, code, instructions, and multimodal data (images, audio) has created a wide range of practical applications.

Content Generation & Writing:

LLMs create blog posts, marketing copy, reports, emails, product descriptions, and creative writing such as stories or scripts. They also improve clarity, tone, and grammar, making them powerful writing assistants.

Customer Support & Virtual Assistants:

LLMs power chatbots, helpdesks, and virtual assistants that can answer questions, troubleshoot issues, and provide personalized support at scale.

Programming & Software Development:

Modern LLMs assist developers by generating code, explaining errors, writing documentation, translating between programming languages, and even suggesting whole functions or algorithms.

Education & Learning:

LLMs help students by explaining difficult concepts, generating study notes, creating quizzes, and offering personalized tutoring experiences.

Research & Knowledge Retrieval:

Researchers use LLMs to summarize papers, extract insights, organize literature, generate hypotheses, and ask natural-language questions over large datasets.

Business Productivity & Automation:

LLMs streamline daily workflows by drafting reports, summarizing meetings, writing proposals, composing emails, and transforming raw information into insights.

Translation & Multilingual Communication:

LLMs support translation between dozens of languages, capturing tone, nuance, and cultural context for clearer communication.

Creative Applications:

LLMs support creative industries by generating story ideas, dialogues, game design concepts, scripts, and even song lyrics.

Industry-Specific Solutions:

LLMs are used across legal, finance, HR, manufacturing, sales, and operations for tasks like document summarization, contract analysis, resume screening, and personalized outreach.

13.8 Summary

- ✓ Transformers revolutionized NLP by introducing **self-attention**, enabling models to process entire sequences and capture long-range dependencies efficiently.
- ✓ Early architectures like **RNNs and LSTMs** struggled with long-term context and parallelization, motivating the development of transformers.
- ✓ Modern LLMs use various transformer configurations:
    - o **Encoder-only models** (BERT) for understanding
    - o **Decoder-only models** (GPT) for text generation
    - o **Encoder–decoder models** (T5) for translation and text transformation
- ✓ LLM training involves four major stages: **tokenization**, **pre-training**, **fine-tuning**, and **RLHF**
- ✓ Prompt engineering plays a crucial role in shaping model behavior, improving accuracy, and guiding output quality.
- ✓ A hands-on project demonstrated how to use a **pre-trained GPT model with PyTorch** to generate text from custom prompts.
- ✓ LLMs have wide real-world applications across content creation, customer support, programming, education, research, translation, and business automation.

Chapter 14: Agentic AI and the Future of Intelligence

14.1 What Is Agentic AI?

Agentic AI represents the next major evolution of artificial intelligence — moving beyond passive models that simply respond to prompts, toward **autonomous agents** that can plan, reason, take actions, and achieve goals with minimal human input.

Traditional AI and LLMs respond to instructions:
"Summarize this text."
"Write a Python script."
"Generate marketing ideas."

Agentic AI goes further. It enables AI systems to:

- Break down goals into smaller tasks
- Decide what actions to take
- Use tools, APIs, and external systems
- Maintain memory and context
- Learn from feedback
- Execute multi-step workflows

In simple words:

Agentic AI = AI that can think + Act, not just respond.

Why Agentic AI is a Big Shift:

While LLMs are powerful, they traditionally behave like "super tools" — useful, but dependent on user instructions.

Agentic AI transforms them into:

- Autonomous assistants
- Digital workers
- Self-directed problem-solvers
- Reasoning engines

Instead of waiting for instructions, an agent can:

- Research a problem
- Form a plan
- Execute tasks step-by-step
- Evaluate outcomes
- Adjust its approach

This opens the door to AI that operates more like a **junior analyst, developer, researcher, or operations assistant**.

Examples of Agentic AI in Action:

Research Agent	Searches the web, Extracts insights, Writes full reports.
Coding Agent	Reads error logs, Debugs code, Tests solutions automatically.
Business Agent	Monitors emails, Updates documents, Notifies the team.
Data Assistant	Load and clean data, Builds visualizations and summaries.

These agents go far beyond simple prompt/response systems — they **operate like digital specialists**.

Why Agentic AI Is Important Now:

Several technological factors make agentic systems possible today:

- Advanced LLM reasoning (GPT, Claude, Gemini)
- Tool usage capabilities (browsers, APIs, code execution)
- Memory systems that allow long-term context
- Orchestration frameworks like LangChain, AutoGen, CrewAI
- Integration with external data sources and applications

This combination allows agents to work independently across real workflows.

Agentic AI vs. Traditional LLMs:

Agentic AI transforms LLMs from passive assistants into **proactive problem solvers**.

Feature	Traditional LLM	Agentic AI
Responds to prompts	Yes	Yes
Multi-step planning	Limited	Strong
Takes autonomous actions	No	Yes
Uses tools & APIs	Limited	Fully
Maintains long-term memory	No/limited	Yes
Works toward goals	No	Yes
Self-correcting	No	Yes

In Summary:

Agentic AI is the future of intelligent systems.

It enables AI to: Plan, Reason, take actions, use tools, work autonomously and achieve long-term goals.

14.2 How AI Agents Plan, Reason and Act Autonomously

A key difference between traditional LLMs and agentic AI is the ability to **plan, reason, and take actions** beyond a single prompt. Instead of simply generating text, agents follow multi-step processes — similar to how a human would solve a problem.

This section explains how autonomous agents think and operate behind the scenes.

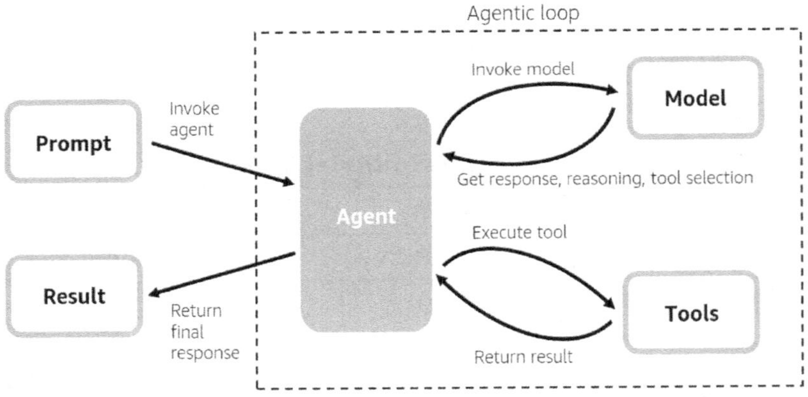

The Agentic AI Loop:

An agentic AI loop is the operating cycle that enables agentic AI systems to move beyond static automation and traditional AI. Instead of reacting only to fixed inputs, the loop integrates reasoning, autonomy, memory, action, and monitoring into a continuous cycle. This allows the system to perceive changing conditions, make autonomous decisions, execute tasks, and adapt based on feedback.

An agent typically follows this repeated cycle:

1. **Plan** – Read the task and break the task into actionable steps
2. **Reason** – Decide what to do next
3. **Act** – Call a tool, run code, search the web, or execute a step
4. **Reflect** – Evaluate the result
5. **Repeat** – Until the goal is completed

This loop continues until the goal is achieved or the agent is stopped.

It's very similar to how humans work:

```
Think → Decide → Act → Evaluate → Continue.
```

1. Planning: *Turning Goals into Steps*

LLMs already possess strong reasoning abilities due to their massive pre-training. Agent frameworks build on this by prompting the model to produce structured plans.

Example Prompt:

```
Goal: Extract customer emails from a PDF.
```

Plan:

1. Load PDF file.
2. Extract text from each page.
3. Find email patterns.
4. Store results in a CSV.

The agent then executes these steps automatically.

2. Reasoning: *Choosing the Best Action*

Reasoning is how an agent decides **which action to take next**.

At this stage, the agent asks itself questions like:

- Do I already have the information I need?
- Should I search for more data?
- Should I call a tool or ask the user for clarification?
- Did my previous step fail?

This reasoning is often powered by:

- Chain-of-thought reasoning
- Structured prompts
- Decision rules
- Feedback from previous actions

Reasoning allows agents to **avoid blind execution** and instead behave thoughtfully.

3. Action: *Interacting with the World*

Actions are how an AI agent affects its environment.

Common actions include:

- Calling APIs
- Searching the web or databases
- Reading or writing files
- Executing code
- Querying vector stores
- Asking the user follow-up questions

Each action produces an **observable result**, which feeds back into the agent loop. This ability to act — not just respond — is what makes agentic AI powerful.

4. Reflect: *Observation and Feedback*

After acting, the agent observes what happened:

- Was the API call successful?
- Did the search return relevant results?
- Did the output meet the goal?

If something goes wrong, the agent can:

- Retry
- Choose a different tool
- Change its strategy
- Ask for clarification

This feedback loop is essential for **robust and adaptive behavior**.

5. Repeat: *Acting Without Constant Human Input*

An AI agent is considered autonomous when it can:

- Continue working without repeated prompts
- Make decisions independently
- Recover from errors
- Stop when the goal is achieved

Autonomy does **not** mean the agent is uncontrolled — humans still:

- Define goals
- Set constraints
- Monitor outcomes

But within those boundaries, the agent can operate on its own.

By combining **planning, reasoning, action, and feedback**, agentic AI systems can handle complexity that single-response AI cannot.

In the next section, we'll look inside an AI agent and break down its **core components** — tools, memory, context, and feedback loops — to understand how these behaviors are implemented in practice.

14.3 Agent Components: Tools, Memory & Context

AI agents are designed to carry out complex tasks autonomously.

After a user provides a high-level goal or prompt, an AI agent decides on the optimal sequence of steps to achieve that goal, using the outcome of each step to inform the next. This capability is enabled by three core components working in tandem:

Model: typically a large language model that serves as the "brain",

Memory: system to retain and recall information, and

Tools: that let the agent interact with external resources or perform actions.

These components form a feedback loop in which the agent plans, acts, and learns from results until it completes the task.

In this section, we'll look at the essential building blocks that make agentic AI possible.

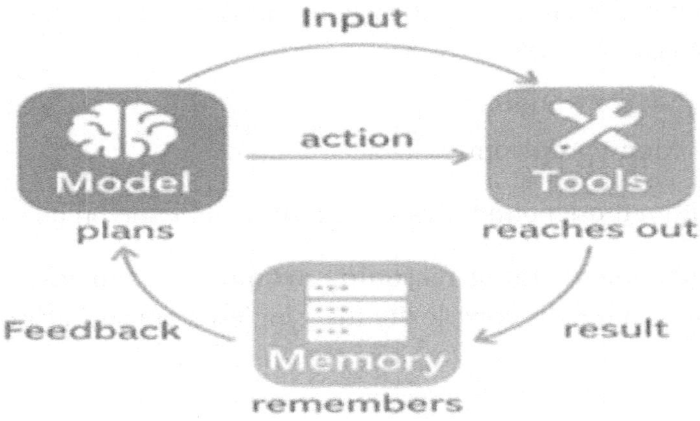

1. Tools — How Agents Take Actions:

Tools are what allow an AI agent to **do things**, not just think.

A tool can be anything the agent can call or interact with, such as:

- APIs (weather, search, payments, databases)
- File systems (read/write documents, PDFs, logs)
- Code execution environments
- Search engines
- Vector databases
- Email or messaging services

Without tools, an agent is limited to generating text. With tools, an agent can **interact with the real world**.

Tools turn LLMs into **action-taking systems**, not just text generators.

2. Memory — The Agent's Knowledge Over Time:

Memory allows an agent to retain information **across steps, tasks, or sessions.**

There are typically two types of memory:

Short-Term Memory

- Holds recent conversation or actions
- Exists only during a single interaction
- Similar to "working memory" in humans

Long-Term Memory

- Stores information for future use
- Can persist across sessions
- Often implemented using databases or vector stores

Memory enables agents to:

- Remember user preferences
- Track progress on long tasks
- Avoid repeating the same mistakes
- Build continuity over time

Without memory, an agent would feel forgetful and unreliable.

3. Context — Understanding the Entire Situation:

Context is the **information the agent uses to make decisions right now**.

Context can include:

- The user's current request and Past interactions
- Retrieved documents
- System instructions
- Tool outputs and Environmental data

The quality of an agent's decisions is directly tied to the **quality and relevance of its context**.

```
Too little context → poor decisions
Too much context → confusion or inefficiency
```

This is why managing context effectively becomes critical as agents grow more complex — a topic we'll explore later when discussing **RAG and MCP**.

4. Feedback Loops — Learning From Success and Failure:

Feedback is what allows AI agents to improve actions over time

Feedback can come from:

- Tool responses (success/error messages)
- User input
- Validation checks
- Internal scoring or rules

For example:

- If a search result is irrelevant → try a different query
- If code execution fails → fix the error and retry
- If the user is unhappy → refine the response

This continuous loop of **act** → **observe** → **adjust** is what gives agents resilience and adaptability.

How These Components Work Together:

An AI agent doesn't use these components in isolation. They work as a system:

1. **Context** informs the agent what's happening
2. **Reasoning** decides what to do next
3. **Tools** execute the action
4. **Feedback** evaluates the result
5. **Memory** stores useful information
6. The cycle repeats

This integrated design is what allows agents to handle multi-step, real-world tasks.

Understanding these components prepares you to build robust autonomous agents in the next sections.

14.4 Agents External Knowledge & Long-Term Memory

Even the most advanced AI agents have an important limitation: **they do not truly "know" everything**. An AI model is trained on a large but **fixed snapshot of data**, and it can only reason within the limits of:

- Its training data
- Its current context window
- The information provided in the prompt

For real-world, long-running, or knowledge-heavy tasks, this is not enough.

The Limits of Model-Only Knowledge:

By default, an AI agent:

- Cannot access private documents
- Cannot see real-time or updated information
- Cannot remember large amounts of past data
- Cannot retain knowledge across sessions

For example, an agent:

- Cannot answer questions about a company's internal PDFs unless it can read them
- Cannot reliably work on large documents that exceed context limits
- Cannot "remember" past interactions unless memory is explicitly added

This is why **external knowledge and long-term memory are essential** for practical agentic systems.

External Knowledge: Expanding What an Agent Can Know:

External knowledge refers to **information stored outside the AI model** that the agent can retrieve when needed.

This can include:

- PDFs, Word documents, and manuals
- Knowledge bases and FAQs
- Databases and logs
- Websites and internal tools
- User-generated content

Instead of relying only on what the model *might* remember from training, the agent can:

- Search
- Retrieve
- Inject relevant information into its reasoning process

This approach makes agents:

- More accurate
- More up-to-date
- More trustworthy
- More useful in business and enterprise settings

Long-Term Memory: Remembering Beyond One Conversation

Long-term memory allows an agent to **retain useful information over time**, beyond a single interaction.

This can include:

- User preferences
- Past decisions
- Task progress; Lessons learned from failures
- Previously retrieved knowledge

With long-term memory, agents feel:

- Consistent instead of forgetful
- Context-aware instead of repetitive
- Intelligent instead of reactive

In practice, long-term memory is often implemented using:

- Databases
- Vector stores
- Persistent storage systems

The key idea is simple:

An agent that cannot remember cannot truly improve.

Why This Leads to RAG and MCP

Once you accept that:

- AI agents need **external knowledge**
- AI agents need **structured, manageable context**
- AI agents need **memory beyond the prompt**

You naturally arrive at two modern solutions:

- **Retrieval-Augmented Generation (RAG)** → focuses on *bringing the right knowledge to the model at the right time*
- **Model Context Protocol (MCP)** → focuses on *managing, organizing, and orchestrating context across tools, agents, and systems*

In the next subsection, we'll start with **RAG**, the most widely used and beginner-friendly approach for giving AI agents access to external knowledge—without retraining models or exceeding context limits.

14.4.1 What Is RAG (Retrieval-Augmented Generation)?

Retrieval-Augmented Generation (RAG) is a technique that allows an AI agent to **look up information from external sources before generating a response**.

Instead of relying only on what the model learned during training, RAG lets the agent:

1. **Retrieve** relevant information from external data
2. **Augment** the model's prompt with that information
3. **Generate** a more accurate, grounded response

In simple terms:

RAG lets AI answer questions using your data, not just its training data.

Why RAG Exists:

Large language models (LLMs) are powerful, but they have three major constraints:

- Their knowledge can be **outdated**
- They cannot access **private or proprietary data**
- They are limited by a **context window**

RAG was created to solve these problems **without retraining the model**.

Instead of changing the model, RAG changes **what the model sees at inference time**.

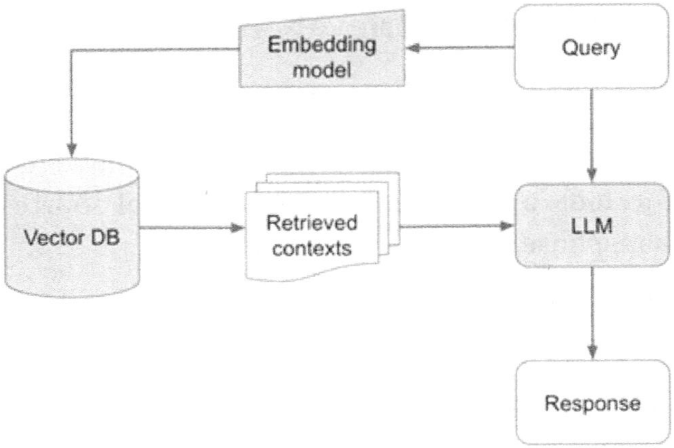

How RAG Works (Step by Step):

A typical RAG pipeline looks like this:

1. **Ingest documents:** PDFs, text files, web pages, manuals, or notes
2. **Chunk the content:** Large documents are split into smaller pieces
3. **Create embeddings:** Each chunk is converted into a numerical representation
4. **Store embeddings:** Stored in a vector database or similar system
5. **User asks a question:** The query is also converted into an embedding
6. **Retrieve relevant chunks:** The most similar pieces of text are fetched from the vector database.
7. **Generate an answer:** The retrieved content is added to the prompt, and the model responds

The model is no longer guessing — it is **grounded in retrieved facts.** In the hands-on project later in this chapter, you'll apply these steps to build a "Chat with Your PDF" RAG system using LangChain and an LLM.

RAG vs Fine-Tuning of Models:

It's important not to confuse RAG with fine-tuning of Models.

Fine-Tuning of Model	RAG
Changes the model	Keeps the model the same
Expensive and slow	Faster and cheaper
Hard to update	Easy to update
Knowledge is "baked in"	Knowledge is retrieved dynamically

For most real-world applications, **RAG is the preferred choice**.

RAG in Agentic Systems:

In an AI agent:

- RAG acts as the **knowledge layer**
- Tools trigger retrieval when needed
- Retrieved content becomes part of the agent's context
- The agent reasons using real data, not assumptions

This makes agents:

- More reliable
- More explainable
- More useful in production systems

RAG's Key Limitation:

While RAG is powerful, it has one limitation:

Context still has to fit inside the model's context window.

As agents grow more complex and start coordinating multiple tools, memories, and workflows, managing context becomes a challenge.

This is where **Model Context Protocol (MCP)** comes in.

In the next subsection, we'll explore **what MCP is, why it exists, and how it differs from RAG** in modern agent architectures.

14.4.2 MCP (Model Context Protocol) vs RAG

As AI agents become more capable, they don't just retrieve documents and answer questions. They:

- Use multiple tools
- Maintain memory
- Coordinate steps across tasks
- Share context between actions (and sometimes between agents)

At this level, **simply retrieving text is not enough**. This is where **Model Context Protocol (MCP)** comes into the picture.

The Problem MCP Tries to Solve:

RAG answers an important question:

"How do we bring the right knowledge into the model?"

But modern agentic systems raise a bigger question:

"How do we manage ***all*** *the context an agent needs—tools, memory, state, and knowledge—without overwhelming the model?"*

An AI agent's context can include:

- Retrieved documents (RAG)
- Tool outputs; Conversation history
- System instructions; Intermediate reasoning
- Memory from past tasks

If all of this is dumped into a single prompt:

- Context windows overflow
- Important information gets lost
- Agent behavior becomes unstable

MCP exists to solve **context orchestration**, not just retrieval.

What Is Model Context Protocol (MCP)?

Model Context Protocol (MCP) is a structured approach to managing, organizing, and delivering **context to AI models in a** controlled way.

Instead of treating context as one large, unstructured prompt, MCP treats it as: Modular, Selective and Purpose-driven.

In simple terms: ***MCP decides what context the model needs right now, and what can be left out.***

A Simple MCP Mental Model:

If RAG is like **searching a library**, then MCP is like a **librarian deciding which books go on your desk**.

- RAG finds relevant information
- MCP decides when, where, and how that information is used
- MCP also manages *non-knowledge context* (tools, state, memory)

What MCP Manages (Beyond RAG):

MCP is not limited to documents. It can manage:

- Tool schemas and tool availability
- Memory summaries instead of raw history
- Task state and progress
- Agent roles and responsibilities
- Multi-agent coordination
- Context prioritization

This makes MCP especially useful for:

- Long-running agents
- Multi-step workflows
- Multi-agent systems
- Enterprise-scale AI applications

MCP vs RAG: Clear Comparison

Aspect	RAG	MCP
Primary purpose	Retrieve external knowledge	Manage and orchestrate context
Focus	Documents & data	Tools, memory, state, knowledge
Scope	Narrow and specific	Broad and system-level
Context size	Still limited	Actively controlled
Replaces the other?	✕ No	✕ No

Key takeaway: RAG and MCP are **complementary**, not competing.

How MCP Fits into Agentic AI

In an agentic system:

- RAG provides **what the agent should know**
- MCP controls **what the agent should see**
- The agent reasons and acts based on **curated context**

Where We Go Next

Now that you understand:

- Why agents need external knowledge
- How RAG brings knowledge into the system
- How MCP manages context at scale

We're ready to look at **frameworks that put all of this into practice**.

In the next section, we'll explore **popular frameworks for building AI agents**, including LangChain, AutoGen, and CrewAI—and how they apply these ideas under the hood.

14.5 Agents Frameworks - LangChain, AutoGen, CrewAI

Understanding agentic AI conceptually is important—but building agents in practice requires **frameworks** that handle planning, tool usage, memory, and context management for you.

In this section, you'll learn about three of the most popular frameworks for agentic AI:

- **LangChain**
- **AutoGen**
- **CrewAI**

Each brings a different approach to building powerful AI-driven workflows.

1. LangChain — The Most Popular Framework for AI Agents

LangChain is one of the earliest and most widely used frameworks for AI agents and RAG-based applications. It provides all the core components needed to build autonomous systems.

What LangChain Is Best At

- Tool integrations (web search, Python, databases, APIs)
- Memory modules (short-term + long-term)
- Chains for multi-step reasoning
- Agents that select tools automatically
- Document loaders and vector databases
- Easy deployment options

This makes it useful for:

- Chatbots with memory
- Knowledge-base assistants
- Data analysts
- Multi-step research agents

Why developers like LangChain: It has strong documentation, many examples, and a gentle learning curve—especially for Python developers.

2. AutoGen — Multi-Agent Cooperation Framework

AutoGen, developed by Microsoft, focuses on enabling **multiple AI agents** to collaborate. Instead of one agent doing everything, AutoGen encourages specialists to work together.

What AutoGen Is Best At

- Multiple agents communicating to each other
- Human-in-the-loop support
- Tool and code execution
- High modularity
- Strong for code generation and debugging

This makes it useful for:

- Code generation and review
- Research assistants
- Multi-step problem solving
- Simulation-style workflows

If LangChain is about *tools and pipelines*, AutoGen is about *teams of agents*.

3. CrewAI — Multi-Agent Teams With Personalities & Roles

CrewAI is designed around the idea of **human-like teams**, where each agent has a clear role and goal.

What CrewAI Is Best At

- Define roles (researcher, writer, planner, developer)
- Agents collaborate like a "crew"
- Built-in memory and tool use
- Supports autonomous workflows
- Ideal for creative or research-heavy tasks

This makes it useful for:

- Business workflows;
- Content pipelines; Structured automation

This multi-agent collaboration mimics human team structures.

Which Framework Should You Use?

Framework	Best For	Key Strength
LangChain	General agent building; production apps	Huge ecosystem, tool-rich
AutoGen	Multi-agent reasoning; coding tasks	Collaboration + accuracy
CrewAI	Team-based creative workflows	Role-based teamwork

How These Frameworks Enable Agentic AI:

These frameworks provide essential features:

- **Tools:** Pre-built modules for Browsers, Python execution, API calls and Databases
- **Memory:** Conversation history, Vector-based long-term memory
- **Planning:** Built-in planner agents, Chain-of-thought decomposition
- **Autonomy:** Run tasks without human supervision, Loops, retries, self-correction
- **Orchestration:** Multi-agent collaboration, Parallel execution, Task coordination

These capabilities make it possible to build fully autonomous AI systems in just a few lines of code.

What You Should Focus on as a Beginner:

You do **not** need to master all frameworks.

A practical learning path:

1. Start with **LangChain**
2. Build a simple agent
3. Add RAG
4. Understand limitations
5. Explore AutoGen or CrewAI later

This approach keeps learning **manageable and rewarding**.

What's Next

Now that you've seen the frameworks that bring agentic AI to life, it's time to **build one yourself**.

In the next section, we'll walk through a **Hands-On : Build Your First Autonomous AI Agent**—step by step, using simple concepts and clean Python code.

14.6 Hands-On: Build Your First Autonomous AI Agent

In this hands-on project, you will build a simple AI agent that can:

1. Take a user query
2. Decide what tools it needs
3. Use those tools to gather information
4. Return a final, thoughtful answer

We'll use **LangChain + OpenAI** to create a basic autonomous research agent.

Goal of the Project:

Build an agent that can automatically:

- Search the web
- Read results
- Summarize insights
- Return a structured answer

Example prompt:

"Research the top 3 cloud certifications and summarize them."

1. Install the Required Libraries:

```
pip install langchain-openai langchain-community langchain
```

2. Create a Simple Research Agent:

Below is the full Python code for an autonomous agent.

Python Code: Build AI Agent

```
# Hands-on Project: Research AI Agent
# langchain_openai is used to access OpenAI chat models
from langchain_openai import ChatOpenAI

# DuckDuckGoSearchRun is a tool that allows web searches
from langchain_community.tools import DuckDuckGoSearchRun
from langchain.agents import create_agent

# Step 1: Setup and assign your OpenAI API Key.
# Note: Do not hard-code API keys in real projects and
# store in an environment variable.

OPENAI_API_KEY = "sk-proj-your-openai-key"

# Step 2: Define the Agent Instructions (System Prompt)

SYSTEM_PROMPT = f"""
You are an autonomous research agent.
You can search the web when needed.
Rules:
- Search first, then write the answer
- Summarize clearly for beginners
- Return a structured answer with:
  - Plan
  - Top 3 findings
  - Final summary
"""
# Step 3: Create the LLM model.
llm = ChatOpenAI(
       model="gpt-5.2",
       temperature=0,
       api_key=OPENAI_API_KEY
       )
```

```
# Step 4: Create the web search tool.
search_tool = DuckDuckGoSearchRun()

# Step 5: Create the AI Agent that can use tools.
agent = create_agent(
        model=llm,
        tools=[search_tool],
        system_prompt=SYSTEM_PROMPT.strip(),
    )

# Step 6: Ask a research question
user_query = "Research the top 3 cloud certifications and
summarize them."

# Step 7: Run the Agent.
Result = agent.invoke(
    {“messages”: [{“role”: “user”, “content”: user_query}]}
    )

# Step 8: Print the agent final response.
print(result["messages"][-1].content)
```

Example Output (Simplified):

Your output may differ, but it will look something like:

```
=== Final Answer ===
Here are the top cloud certifications in 2026:

• AWS Solutions Architect – Associate
  - Strong job demand
  - Updated exam based on cloud best practices

• Microsoft Azure Administrator (AZ-104)
  - Highly valued for enterprise cloud management
  - Covers identity, governance, networking

• Google Professional Cloud Architect
  - Strong salary growth
  - Ideal for multi-cloud environments
```

The key point: **The AI Agent researched, verified, and summarized the info automatically.**

What You Learned in project:

By completing this project, you now understand how to:

- Build a basic autonomous agent
- Add tools that allow real actions
- Run multi-step tasks automatically
- Use LangChain for real-world agent workflows

This is the foundation of all advanced agentic systems.

14.7 The Future: AI + Robotics + Edge Computing

Agentic AI is the foundation of next-generation intelligent systems. Its true potential emerges when combined with **robotics** and **edge computing**. Together, these three pillars are shaping the future of intelligence.

From Digital to Physical Agents:

Previously, we focused on software agents that read documents, answer questions, and automate workflows.

The next step is **embodiment**—AI agents that can:

- **Sense** the physical world
- **Decide** in real time
- **Act** physically

This is where **robotics** provides the "body" for the AI "brain." Examples include:

- **Warehouse robots** coordinating tasks autonomously.
- **Delivery robots** navigating dynamic environments.
- **Industrial robots** adapting to changing conditions.
- **Home assistants** responding intelligently to context.

Why Edge Computing Matters:

Traditional AI relies on cloud infrastructure, which faces limitations in latency, network dependency, privacy, and bandwidth costs.

Edge computing brings AI closer to data sources like sensors, cameras, and IoT devices. For agentic AI, this enables:

- **Instant responsiveness** and faster decision-making.
- **Enhanced privacy** and data security.
- **Offline operation** without constant cloud access.

An edge agent can **Sense** → **Reason** → **Act** instantly, maintaining functionality even in low-connectivity environments.

The Convergence: AI Agents at the Edge:

When agentic AI, robotics, and edge computing converge, systems become **autonomous, adaptive, context-aware, and resilient.**

For example, an edge-based agent might monitor machinery, detect local abnormalities, reason through potential failures, and trigger preventive action—syncing with the cloud only when necessary.

This creates **distributed intelligence** rather than centralized control.

Looking Ahead:

The synergy of these technologies will define the next era of:

- Smart cities and autonomous industries.
- Intelligent healthcare systems.
- Adaptive digital assistants.

14.8 Hands-On: Build your RAG AI Agent - PDF Q&A Chatbot using LangChain and OpenAI

This final project brings together everything you've learned in this chapter. You'll build a **Retrieval-Augmented Generation (RAG) AI agent** that can read a PDF document and answer questions about it—one of the most practical and popular real-world applications of agentic AI.

What You'll Build

By the end of this project, you'll have an AI system that can:

- Load a PDF document
- Break it into readable chunks
- Store its content for retrieval
- Accept user questions
- Retrieve relevant sections from the PDF
- Generate accurate answers grounded in the document

In short: **You'll build a "Chat with Your PDF" AI agent using RAG.**

How This Uses Agentic AI Concepts

This project demonstrates:

- **Agent behavior** – the system decides how to answer
- **External knowledge** – the PDF is not part of the model's training
- **RAG** – relevant content is retrieved before answering
- **Tools** – document loaders, embeddings, and retrievers
- **Context management** – only relevant text is sent to the model

This is a realistic example of how agentic AI is used in businesses today.

RAG PIPELINE:

```
[PDF] → LOAD → SPLIT → EMBED → STORE [Chroma DB]
   ↑                            ↓

"Question?" ← RETRIEVE ← SIMILARITY SEARCH

                        ↓

                LLM + Context → ANSWER
```

Install Required Libraries

```
pip install langchain langchain-community langchain-openai
pip install langchain-text-splitters langchain-chroma
pip install pypdf chromadb
```

Step 1: Import all libraires

```
from langchain_community.document_loaders import PyPDFLoader
from langchain_text_splitters import RecursiveCharacterTextSplitter
from langchain_openai import OpenAIEmbeddings, ChatOpenAI
from langchain_chroma import Chroma
from langchain_core.tools import tool
from langchain.agents import create_agent
```

Libraries	Detail
PyPDFLoader	Extracts text from PDF files
RecursiveCharacterTextSplitter	Splits large text into chunks
OpenAIEmbeddings	Converts text to vectors for similarity search
ChatOpenAI	OpenAI GPT chat model
Chroma	Vector database stores embeddings for search
@tool decorator	Turns Python functions into tools
create_agent	Builds autonomous agents

Step 2: Setup and assign your OpenAI API Key.

```
# Note: Do not hard-code API keys in real projects and
# store in an environment variable.

OPENAI_API_KEY = "sk-proj-your-openai-key"
```

Step 3: Load PDF file (replace with your PDF path)

```
loader = PyPDFLoader("your-document.pdf")
docs = loader.load()
```

Step 4: Split the Document into Chunks

Large documents must be split into smaller chunks.

```
text_splitter = RecursiveCharacterTextSplitter(
                    chunk_size=1000,
                    chunk_overlap=200)

chunks = text_splitter.split_documents(docs)
```

Step 5: Create Embeddings and Vector Store

Embeddings convert text into numerical form and store them into a vector database like chroma.

```
embeddings = OpenAIEmbeddings(api_key=OPENAI_API_KEY)
vectorstore = Chroma.from_documents(
    documents=chunks,
    embedding=embeddings,
    persist_directory="./chroma_db" # Saves locally for reuse
   )
retriever = vectorstore.as_retriever()
```

Step 6: Create retriever tool

Searches and returns excerpts from the uploaded PDF relevant to the query.

```
@tool
def search_pdf(query: str) -> str:
    docs = retriever.invoke(query)
    return "\n\n".join(doc.page_content for doc in docs)

pdf_tools = [search_pdf]
```

Step 7: Create OpenAI chat model

```
llm = ChatOpenAI(model="gpt-5.2",
                 temperature=0,
                 api_key=OPENAI_API_KEY)
```

Step 8: Create agent with tools and system prompt

```
SYSTEM_PROMPT = """You are a helpful assistant that answers
questions about the PDF document. Use the search_pdf tool
whenever you need information from the document.
If you cannot find the answer in the PDF, say so clearly."""

agent = create_agent(model=llm,
                     tools=pdf_tools,
                     system_prompt=SYSTEM_PROMPT.strip())
```

Step 9: Ask Questions to Chatbot about PDF. User can exit by typing exit or quit.

```
# Interactive query loop
while True:
    query = input("Question: ")
    if query.lower() in ['quit', 'exit']:
        break

    response = agent.invoke(
            {"messages": [{"role": "user", "content": query}]})

    print(response["messages"][-1].content)
```

Example Output:

`Question:` `Can we please summarize the document?`

`Agent:` `The document discusses [topic] on pages 3-5...`

The AI Agent:

1. Reads System_Prompt + Question
2. Searches the PDF content from Vector database (search_pdf tool)
3. Finds relevant sections
4. GPT answers based on the document (Question + Context)

Complete Code: "Chat with Your PDF" AI agent using RAG.

```
# Step 1: Import all libraires

from langchain_community.document_loaders import PyPDFLoader
from langchain_text_splitters import RecursiveCharacterTextSplitter
from langchain_openai import OpenAIEmbeddings, ChatOpenAI
from langchain_chroma import Chroma
from langchain_core.tools import tool
from langchain.agents import create_agent

# Step 2: Setup and assign your OpenAI API Key.

# Note: Do not hard-code API keys in real projects and
# store in an environment variable.

OPENAI_API_KEY = "sk-proj-your-openai-key"

# Step 3: Load PDF file (replace with your PDF path)

loader = PyPDFLoader("your-document.pdf")
docs = loader.load()

# Step 4: Split the Document into Chunks

text_splitter = RecursiveCharacterTextSplitter(
                    chunk_size=1000,chunk_overlap=200)

chunks = text_splitter.split_documents(docs)

# Step 5: Create Embeddings and Vector Store

embeddings = OpenAIEmbeddings(api_key=OPENAI_API_KEY)
vectorstore = Chroma.from_documents(
  documents=chunks,
  embedding=embeddings,
  persist_directory="./chroma_db"  # Saves locally for reuse
 )

retriever = vectorstore.as_retriever()
```

```
# Step 6: Create retriever tool

@tool
def search_pdf(query: str) -> str:
    docs = retriever.invoke(query)
    return "\n\n".join(doc.page_content for doc in docs)

pdf_tools = [search_pdf]

# Step 7: Create OpenAI chat model

llm = ChatOpenAI(model="gpt-5.2",
                 temperature=0,
                 api_key=OPENAI_API_KEY)

# Step 8: Create agent with tools and system prompt

SYSTEM_PROMPT = """You are a helpful assistant that answers
questions about the PDF document. Use the search_pdf tool
whenever you need information from the document.
If you cannot find the answer in the PDF, say so clearly."""

agent = create_agent(model=llm,
                     tools=pdf_tools,
                     system_prompt=SYSTEM_PROMPT.strip())


# Step 9: Ask Questions to Chatbot about PDF.
# User can exit by typing exit or quit.
# Interactive query loop

while True:
   query = input("Question: ")
   if query.lower() in ['quit', 'exit']:
       break

   response = agent.invoke(
          {"messages": [{"role": "user", "content": query}]})

   print(response["messages"][-1].content)
```

Summary of What You Accomplished:

By completing this AI Agent project, you learned how to:

- Load and process PDF documents
- Split large text into searchable chunks
- Create embeddings and store them in a vector database
- Retrieve relevant information for a user question
- Provide context to an AI model for grounded answers

14.9 Summary

In this chapter, you explored how AI is evolving from passive models into **agentic systems** that can plan, reason, act, and adapt.

You learned:

- How autonomous agents operate using planning and feedback loops
- Why tools, memory, and context are critical
- How RAG gives agents access to external knowledge
- How MCP helps manage context as systems scale
- How frameworks like LangChain, AutoGen, and CrewAI support agent development

Through hands-on projects, you built both an autonomous agent and a RAG-based document assistant—demonstrating how agentic AI is applied in real-world systems today.

You are no longer just **using AI**. You are now thinking like someone who **builds intelligent systems**.

Chapter 15:
Final Summary & Next Steps

Congratulations — by reaching this final chapter, you've completed a comprehensive journey through the world of Artificial Intelligence, Machine Learning, Deep Learning, Generative AI, Large Language Models, and Agentic AI.

By now, you've moved from Python fundamentals to building intelligent, agentic AI systems—an achievement that puts you well ahead of most professionals.

15.1 What You've Learned in This Book

This book took you on a complete journey through modern AI development.

You started by building a strong foundation in **Python**, learning to:

- Work with data structures, control flow, and functions
- Use NumPy, Pandas, and Matplotlib for data handling and visualization
- Write clean, reusable Python code for AI applications

You then explored **machine learning**, where you learned to:

- Understand supervised and unsupervised learning
- Train, evaluate, and compare ML models
- Apply regression, classification, clustering, and dimensionality reduction
- Build end-to-end ML projects using real datasets

Next, you moved into **deep learning**, learning:

- How neural networks work
- How to build and train models with TensorFlow and Keras
- How CNNs and RNNs handle images and sequential data

Finally, you stepped into **modern AI systems**, including:

- **Generative AI** and large language models
- Transformers and prompt engineering
- **Agentic AI** systems that plan, reason, and act
- Retrieval-Augmented Generation (RAG) for working with real data
- Model Context Protocol (MCP) for managing complex context
- Frameworks like LangChain, AutoGen, and CrewAI
- Hands-on projects that reflect how AI is used in production today

By the end of this book, you didn't just learn isolated techniques—you learned how **AI systems are designed, built, and applied end to end**.

In Summary:

By completing this book, you have gained:

✓ **A strong foundation in Python**
✓ **A deep understanding of ML and DL**
✓ **Practical skills with AI frameworks**
✓ **Knowledge of modern LLMs and Generative AI**
✓ **Hands-on experience building real AI projects**
✓ **The ability to build autonomous AI agents**
✓ **The confidence to build your own AI applications**

You now have everything needed to begin your journey as an AI developer.

15.2 Building Your Own AI Projects

The most effective way to grow in AI is by building your own projects.

When starting a new AI project, think in terms of **systems**, not models:

1. Identify a real problem worth solving
2. Decide how AI adds value (prediction, generation, automation, decision support)
3. Choose the right data source (files, databases, APIs, user input)
4. Start with a simple baseline solution
5. Improve accuracy, reliability, and usability step by step

Good project ideas include:

- AI assistants for documents or knowledge bases
- Automation tools for repetitive workflows
- Data analysis and insight-generation systems
- Research or summarization agents
- Domain-specific chatbots

Remember: strong AI projects are built through **iteration**, not perfection on the first attempt.

1. Decide the Role of AI in Your System:

Define how AI fits into your project:

- **Predictor** – forecasts values or trends
- **Classifier** – assigns categories
- **Generator** – creates text, images, or summaries
- **Agent** – plans, reasons, and takes actions
- **Assistant** – supports users with automation or insights

This decision guides your choice of models and tools.

2. Choose the Right Data Source:

Data is the foundation of every AI project. Common data sources include:

Public datasets

- **Kaggle** – real-world datasets for ML practice
- **UCI Machine Learning Repository** – classic, well-curated datasets
- **Hugging Face Datasets** – text, image, and audio datasets
- **Google Dataset Search** – discover open datasets

Private or custom data

- PDFs and documents
- Company reports and logs
- User-generated data
- APIs and live data streams

Start with small, clean datasets before scaling.

3. Build a Simple Baseline First:

Always begin with a minimal working solution:

- One dataset
- One model or workflow
- One clear output

This helps you validate your idea quickly and avoid unnecessary complexity.

4. Think in Pipelines, Not Scripts

As projects grow, structure them as pipelines:

- Data ingestion → processing → output
- Retrieve → reason → generate
- Input → tools → response

This approach makes it easier to extend your system with agents, memory, or additional tools later.

5. Deploy Your AI Project:

Deployment turns a project into a usable system.

Common deployment options include:

Local or simple demos:

- Jupyter Notebook
- Google Colab

Cloud platforms:

- **AWS** (EC2, Lambda, SageMaker)
- **Azure** (App Service, Azure ML)
- **Google Cloud Platform**
- **Hugging Face Spaces** for demos

Web application deployment:

- Backend APIs using FastAPI or Flask
- Frontends using simple web frameworks
- Containerization with Docker

Choose deployment based on:

- Project complexity
- Expected users
- Cost and scalability needs

6. Test, Improve, and Iterate

Once deployed:

- Test with real inputs
- Monitor failures and edge cases
- Improve prompts, models, or data
- Add safeguards and explanations

Iteration is what turns experiments into reliable systems.

15.3 Exploring Career Opportunities in AI

The field of Artificial Intelligence is one of the fastest-growing, highest-paying, and most future-proof industries in the world. Companies across every sector — technology, healthcare, finance, retail, aviation, education, and even government — are rapidly adopting AI.

AI Is a Cross-Disciplinary Field:

One of the most important things to understand about AI careers is that AI is not a single job role.

AI intersects with:

- Software development
- Data analysis
- Cloud computing
- Product design
- Business operations
- Automation and decision-making

This means you can work in AI **without** being a mathematician or research scientist.

What Companies Look for in AI Roles:

Most employers value practical skills over theory alone.

Common expectations include:

- Understanding how AI and ML systems work
- Ability to work with data and models
- Experience using AI frameworks and APIs
- Building end-to-end AI applications
- Evaluating outputs for accuracy and reliability
- Awareness of ethical and responsible AI use

Your hands-on experience with projects is a major advantage. Projects like document-based Q&A systems, autonomous agents, or data-driven predictors are often more impressive than certificates alone.

Industries Hiring AI Talent:

AI skills are in demand across many industries, including:

- Technology and software
- Finance and banking
- Healthcare and life sciences
- E-commerce and retail
- Marketing and content creation
- Manufacturing and logistics
- Education and research

In many cases, companies are not hiring "AI experts" specifically—they are hiring **engineers, analysts, and developers who understand AI**.

Entry Points Into AI Careers:

You can enter the AI field from multiple starting points:

- **Software developers** adding AI capabilities to applications
- **Data analysts** moving into predictive and intelligent systems
- **Cloud engineers** deploying and managing AI workloads
- **Automation specialists** enhancing workflows with AI agents

Your existing skills become more valuable when combined with AI knowledge.

15.4 Career Paths & Opportunities in AI

AI offers a wide range of career paths, each focusing on different aspects of building, deploying, and applying intelligent systems. You don't need to master every area—most professionals specialize while building on a shared foundation of AI knowledge.

Below are some of the most common and realistic AI career paths you can explore.

1. AI / Machine Learning Engineer:

AI and Machine Learning Engineers focus on building, integrating, and deploying AI models into real applications.

Typical responsibilities include:

- Training and evaluating ML models
- Integrating models into software systems
- Working with APIs, data pipelines, and cloud platforms
- Improving model performance and reliability

This role suits people with strong Python skills and an interest in applying models in production environments.

2. Data Scientist / Data Analyst:

Data Scientists and Analysts use AI and ML to extract insights from data and support decision-making.

Common tasks include:

- Data exploration and visualization
- Building predictive and analytical models
- Interpreting results for business or technical teams
- Communicating insights clearly

This path is ideal if you enjoy working with data, patterns, and analysis.

3. AI Solutions Architect:

AI Solutions Architects design end-to-end AI systems rather than individual models. They focus on:

- Choosing appropriate AI approaches and tools
- Designing scalable and maintainable architectures
- Integrating AI with existing systems
- Balancing performance, cost, and reliability

This role often combines AI knowledge with cloud, system design, and business understanding.

4. Automation Engineer / AI Engineer for Workflows:

Automation-focused roles use AI to streamline repetitive tasks and processes. Examples include:

- Intelligent document processing
- Workflow automation using AI agents
- Customer support automation
- Data processing and reporting pipelines

This role is ideal if you enjoy improving efficiency and building practical tools.

5. AI Application Developer:

AI Application Developers focus on user-facing AI systems.

They typically:

- Build chatbots, assistants, and AI-powered apps
- Integrate LLMs, RAG, and agents into products
- Work closely with frontend or product teams
- Focus on usability and user experience

This path is a strong fit for software developers expanding into AI.

6. AI Consultant or Technical Specialist:

AI Consultants help organizations understand and adopt AI effectively.

They may:

- Evaluate AI readiness and use cases
- Design proof-of-concept systems
- Advise on tools, platforms, and strategies
- Bridge technical and business teams

This role rewards communication skills alongside technical knowledge.

Combining AI With Your Existing Skills:

Many successful AI professionals do not start in AI.

AI pairs well with:

- Software development
- Cloud and DevOps
- Finance, healthcare, or domain expertise
- Research and education
- Product management

Combining AI with another specialization often creates **stronger and more unique career profiles**.

Key Takeaway:

The most successful professionals build on their existing strengths, apply AI where it creates value, and continue learning as the field evolves.

The skills you've developed in this book give you a solid foundation to explore these paths with confidence.

15.5 Continuing Your Learning Journey

Artificial intelligence is one of the fastest-moving fields in the world. New tools, models, and breakthroughs emerge constantly.

Becoming successful in AI is not about mastering everything once—it's about **continuous learning, hands-on practice, and staying curious**. This section provides a clear roadmap to help you keep growing long after finishing this book.

1. Keep Building Projects — The Most Powerful Way to Learn

The most effective way to improve your AI skills is by continuing to build projects, such as:

- Chatbots and LLM-based applications
- Multi-agent systems
- Generative AI tools
- Automation workflows
- Deep learning models

Each project you build deepens your understanding far more than passive study.

2. Explore New AI Subfields

AI is a broad and rapidly expanding domain. After this book, you may choose to specialize further in areas such as:

Advanced Deep Learning

- Transformers
- Vision transformers
- Diffusion models

Computer Vision

- Object detection, Image segmentation, Face recognition

NLP & LLMs

- Fine-tuning large models
- Building domain-specific LLMs

Generative AI

- AI image and video generation
- Text-to-audio and music models

Agentic AI

- Multi-agent collaboration
- Tool-based autonomous systems
- Integrating agents with robots or APIs

The possibilities for growth are virtually unlimited.

3. Practice on Real Platforms:

Hands-on experience accelerates learning faster than anything else. Strong platforms to practice include:

Kaggle

- Competitions
- Datasets
- Notebooks

Hugging Face Spaces

- Deploy AI models
- Explore open-source LLMs

GitHub

- Publish projects
- Contribute to AI libraries

Consistent practice on real platforms helps transform knowledge into confidence.

4. Consider Certifications:

If you're pursuing **cloud-based AI roles**, certifications can be a valuable complement to your skills.

Cloud platforms such as AWS, Azure, and Google Cloud play a major role in modern AI deployments. To support certification preparation—especially for cloud exams—you can use **MyCloudCertification.com**, a platform designed to help learners practice certification-style questions and strengthen their technical understanding.

It's particularly useful for preparing for:

- Azure certifications
- AWS certifications
- Google Cloud certifications
- AI-focused cloud specializations

Used alongside hands-on projects, certifications can help validate your knowledge and career readiness.

Your AI Journey Starts Now:

By completing this book, you now have:

- ✓ A strong foundation in Python, Machine Learning and Deep Learning
- ✓ Practical experience with GenAI, LLMs, and Agentic AI systems
- ✓ Hands-on project experience that employer's value
- ✓ Skills to build applications from idea → deployment
- ✓ A clear roadmap for continued growth

The world is entering a new era powered by AI — and you now have the skills to be part of it. **This is just the beginning.**

*****Congratulations! — You've Completed the Book*****

You are now equipped to:

- Build intelligent systems
- Create AI-powered applications
- Design agentic workflows
- Solve real-world problems
- Pursue a professional AI career
- Shape the future of technology

The next step is yours: **Go build something amazing**.

AUTHOR'S NOTE:

Thank you for taking the time to read this book.

Artificial intelligence can feel overwhelming at first, but its true power lies not in complexity, but in thoughtful application. My goal in writing this book was to guide you from fundamentals to real-world systems, helping you build confidence along the way.

If you take one thing from this journey, let it be this: progress comes from building. Keep experimenting, keep refining your ideas, and don't be afraid to start small.

AI is a rapidly evolving field, but the ability to think clearly, design reliable systems, and apply technology responsibly will always matter.

I wish you curiosity, patience, and success as you continue your journey in AI.

— Ghulam Mustafa —

ABOUT THE AUTHOR

Ghulam Mustafa is a Senior Software Engineer and Cloud Solutions engineer with extensive experience in cloud computing, software development and artificial intelligence. He helps individuals and businesses build scalable cloud architectures, AI-powered applications, and modern automation solutions. With a passion for teaching, he simplifies complex technical topics so readers at any skill level can learn quickly and build confidently. He is also the founder of **VertixCloud**, a UK-based Cloud and AI services provider.

ABOUT VERTIXCLOUD

VertixCloud is a UK-based technology brand specializing in cloud computing, artificial intelligence, and modern automation solutions. The company helps individuals and businesses adopt scalable cloud architectures, integrate AI into real-world applications, and upskill through practical, hands-on learning resources.

VertixCloud offers services that include cloud infrastructure consulting, AI model development, automation workflows, developer training, and educational content focused on Python, machine learning, cloud technologies, and modern GenAI systems.

With a mission to make advanced technology accessible, VertixCloud supports learners and professionals at every stage—whether they're exploring AI for the first time, building production-ready systems, or scaling solutions in the cloud.

To learn more, visit: **VertixCloud.com**

Made in the USA
Monee, IL
04 November 2026

67384799R00125